Robert Burns

AND THE HELLISH LEGION

Tam tint his reason a' thegither,
And roars out, 'Weel done, Cutty-sark!'
And in an instant all was dark!
And scarcely had he Maggie rallied,
When out the hellish legion sallied.

— TAM O' SHANTER —

Robert Burns

AND THE HELLISH LEGION

JOHN BURNETT

National Museums Scotland

Published in 2009 by
NMS Enterprises Limited – Publishing
a division of NMS Enterprises Limited
National Museums Scotland
Chambers Street
Edinburgh EH1 1JF

Text © Trustees of National Museums Scotland 2009

www.nms.ac.uk

ISBN: 978 1 905267 31 6

Publication layout and design by
    NMS Enterprises Limited – Publishing.
Cover design by Mark Blackadder. The cover image of Robert
    Burns is from *Cassell's Old and New Edinburgh: Its History,
    its People and its Places* by James Grant (Cassell & Co. Ltd:
    London, Paris, New York and Melbourne, no date). The
    background image is from *Tam O'Shanter* by Robert Burns,
    'published for the members of the Royal association for the
    promotion of the fine arts in Scotland' (Edinburgh: 1855).
Printed and bound in Great Britain
    by Athenaeum Press Ltd, Gateshead, Tyne & Wear.

For a full listing of NMS Enterprises Limited – Publishing titles
and related merchandise:

www.nms.ac.uk/books

Contents

Acknowledgements

ONE of the benefits of working in National Museums Scotland is the range of colleagues who have specialist enthusiasm and knowledge, and it is a pleasure to name those who have helped: Dr David Caldwell, George Dalgleish, Elaine Edwards, Dr Godfrey Evans, David Forsyth, Dorothy Kidd, Kate MacKay, Katherine Mercer, Lesley Taylor and Chris Waddell.

Other professionals who gave of their time and expertise are Kenneth Dunn and Olive Geddes of the National Library of Scotland; Tom Barclay and his colleagues at the Carnegie Library, Ayr; Helen McArthur and Graham Roberts of the Ewart Library, Dumfries; and at the National Archives of Scotland, Dr David Brown, Dr Tristram Clarke and Robin Urquhart.

Two Ayrshire historians, Rob Close and Sheriff David B. Smith, shared their knowledge of the history of the county, and the latter also his command of Ayrshire Scots.

The text, in whole or in part, was read by Marguerita Burnett, Dr Gerard Carruthers, Prof. Sandy Fenton, David Forsyth, Kate MacKay, Dr Malcolm Nicolson, Sheriff David B. Smith, Gavin Sprott and Lesley Taylor: they found errors and solecisms, and made welcome improvements. Any remaining faults in fact or judgement are the responsibility of the author.

The final process of turning ragged text into a finished book was carried though by a team which included Maggie Wilson and Kate Blackadder, and Kate MacKay who wrote the captions for the illustrations and the note on Thomas Bewick.

As Robert Burns wrote to William Simpson of Ochiltree, 'wi grateful heart I thank you brawlie'.

John Burnett, 2009

Image and Text Credits

DUMFRIES MUSEUM
(© Dumfries Museum)

for art section – *figs* 1, 2, 9, 18, 22

EDINBURGH UNIVERSITY LIBRARY
(© Edinburgh University Library: Centre for Research Collections)

for art section – *fig.* 12

NATIONAL GALLERIES OF SCOTLAND
(© The Trustees of the National Galleries of Scotland)

NATIONAL GALLERY OF SCOTLAND
for art section – *fig.* 6 (Alexander Runciman/'The Witches show Macbeth the Apparitions'); *fig.* 11 (John Faed/'Tam o' Shanter'); *fig.* 26 (Thomas Stothard/'The Deil's awa wi the Exciseman')

SCOTTISH NATIONAL PORTRAIT GALLERY
fig. 17 (Alexander Reid/Robert Burns); *fig.* 21 (Alexander Carse/ Self Portrait)

NATIONAL LIBRARY OF SCOTLAND
(© Reproduced by kind permission of the Trustees of the National Library of Scotland)

for art section – *figs* 15, 24; and the Bewick engravings from *The Poetical Works of Robert Burns* (1808) – for pp III, 1, 13, 28, 37, 57, 71, 84, 99

NATIONAL MUSEUMS SCOTLAND
(© National Museums Scotland)

for art section – *figs* 4, 5, 8, 10, 13, 14, 16, 19, 25, 27, 29, 30, 31

NATIONAL TRUST FOR SCOTLAND
(© Reproduced by kind permission of the National Trust for Scotland)

for art section – *figs* 7, 20, 23, 28; *fig.* 32 (John Sinclair)

UNIVERSITY OF GLASGOW
(© University of Glasgow/James Taylor, *The Pictorial History of Scotland, from the Roman Invasion to the close of the Jacobite Rebellion AD79-1746*, 2 vols [London: James S. Vitue 1859], vol. 2, p. 712. Licensor www.scran.ac.uk)

for art section – *fig.* 3

With thanks to Jenni Calder for permission to quote from David Daiches (1966): *Robert Burns: the Poet* (2nd ed.) on pp. 11, 65 and 113 of this book.

Preface

R OBERT Burns[1] was on home ground when he wrote 'The Brigs of Ayr', linking his own creativity with the supernatural.

That Bards are second-sighted is nae joke,
And ken the lingo of the sp'ritual folk;
Fays, Spunkies, Kelpies, a', they can explain them,
An ev'n the very deils they brawly ken them.[2]

The purpose of this book is to explore some aspects of life in the world in which Burns lived and wrote. It looks at the supernatural beliefs which people held, and how they fitted into their lives.

It is written in the conviction that, until recent decades, Scottish history has been seen as taking place in a country peopled by politicians, soldiers, lawyers and ministers, who over the span of time have mostly been men. The rest of the people – men and women – the hidden nine-tenths – deserve nine-tenths of the history, whether they were watching the sky over the fishing grounds, washing clothes in the burn, taking a sickle to the corn in the harvest field, or sitting at the fireside, telling the story about a witch pursuing a drunken farmer on a grey horse. Folk tales and beliefs are as important a part of cultural history as novels or organised religion.

Robert Burns and the Hellish Legion describes some of the networks of ideas and physical objects, actions and activities, which expressed the values of the people in the fields or by the fireside, the ways in which they judged the world they could see, hear, taste, smell and touch. It sees Burns in the context of the beliefs and fears of the people around him. He believed in the supernatural in as far as it was part of his Christian religion. He did not believe that the Devil, horned and cloven-hoofed, appeared in Ayrshire, or that witches existed and had supernatural powers. He understood, however, that other people did think that Satan walked the earth and that witches were real, and that these were not blind, pointless traditions, but genuine feelings which stemmed from the need to understand the inconsistent world.

John Burnett, 2009

NOTES

1 William Burnes, the father of Robert Burns, spelled his name with an 'e'. Robert removed the 'e' when he became an adult, and in this publication the more familiar spelling has been applied over the whole of his life.

2 Robertson (1904), p. 46; Kinsley (1968), p. 284. The quotations from the work of Robert Burns used in this publication are from J. Logie Robertson's edition, and reference is also given to James Kinsley's scholarly edition.

A NOTE ON
Thomas Bewick

THOMAS BEWICK, 1753-1828, was born the son of a farmer, at Cherryburn, about 20 miles from Newcastle. His passion for the countryside and its natural history lasted throughout his life, and was matched by his enthusiasm for drawing, these two elements coming together to great effect in the many hundreds of matchless wood engravings he made.

Apprenticed at the age of 14 to the only engraver in Newcastle, Bewick later went into partnership with his master, and concentrated on the commissions for wood engravings, many of them to illustrate small books for children. His books on quadrupeds and birds established his reputation, and working on the tailpiece vignettes was the work he enjoyed most.

In a list of Bewick's library compiled in 1806 by his daughter Jane, there are several copies of Burns's poems, as well as R. H. Cromek's *Select Scottish Songs … with critical observations and biographical notices by Robert Burns* (1810), and also his *Reliques of Robert Burns* (1808). The poet was evidently popular in the household.

For *The Poetical Works of Robert Burns* (1808), the source of the illustrations at the beginning of each chapter in this volume, Bewick and his apprentices engraved from designs by John Thurston, an artist born in Yorkshire but who had lived in Newcastle as a child.

The owl on the title page conjures up 'Ye houlets, frae your ivy bower, / In some auld tree, or eldritch tower …' from Burns's 'Elegy on Captain Matthew Henderson'. Solitary and nocturnal owls are commonly associated with the supernatural, and are often shown as the companions of witches. Their screeching unearthly calls were thought to herald death, and to see one in daylight was a bad omen.

Bewick's owl shows the skills of the engraver at their finest.

Kate MacKay

CHAPTER 1

INTRODUCTION

The Life of Robert Burns

ROBERT Burns was born in 1759 in the 'auld clay biggin' that his father had made at Alloway.[1] William Burnes built his house out of Ayrshire soil, hard-packed. A piece of the body of the wall can still be seen to this day, with straw in the earth to make it bind better. Robert was born on earth – and he was born in earth, surrounded by it, surrounded by the source, along with the Sun, of all life.

When his plough destroyed the nest of a mouse, he told the bereft animal that he was his 'poor, earth-born companion'. Earth, here, has two meanings – the planet and the maternal clay. The earth had the power to make things grow and flourish, particularly if it was well-tended and there were no exceptional events such as a plague among the cattle or prolonged bad weather. A young woman teased the 16-year-old Burns, telling him that he should not be looking down, but at her and her sister. Did he admit to shyness, or that he was lost in his own thoughts? His reply was more profound: 'It is a natural and right thing for a man to contemplate the ground from which he was taken.'[2]

When a farmer wanted to decide whether the spring earth was warm enough to be ploughed, he dropped his trousers and sat on it. The earth told him. In the Highlands a man was selected in each village to manage the collective work such as cutting peat and carrying it home, representing the people in their dealings with their landlord, and so on. When he accepted this role there was a ceremony in which he stood barefoot on 'the earth of which he was made and to which he would return, and lifting his eyes to heaven promised that he would act fairly'.[3] In Greek mythology the giant Antaeus was strong as long as he was in contact with mother earth; in Roman legend Horatius was drowning until his feet touched the river bed, revitalising him; similarly, when Robert Bruce's fortunes were at their worst he retreated into the earth and lived in a cave. The life-giving earth was the home of non-human beings such as fairies, who lived underground, and some kinds of bees which built their hives there. An old couplet said that when land is brought under cultivation, the friendly spirits and bees departed:

Where the scythe cuts, and the sock rives [ploughshare tears open]
Hae done wi' fairies and bee-bykes.[4] [hives]

The midwife at Robert's birth was probably Agnes McClure, wife of the local blacksmith. The smith was a man of high standing in the community because he was the only person in the parish who could work hot metal – he could make things which no one else could make – and as an extension of one skill, smiths were often believed to have the power of healing. By association, their wives were able to help with women's health and childbirth.

When Robert was seven years old, the Burnes family moved from the low ground at Alloway to Mount Oliphant, half-way up a stark hillside, and they stayed there for eleven years. A commentator wrote that in this area 'part of the soil is fertile, and part barren; part of it deep, and part shallow'.[5] The soil at Mount Oliphant was barren and shallow: it was bone with little flesh on it.

In one Ayrshire parish it was said that most people kept a cow or two, and two or three sheep. Selling a year-old calf for 30 to 50 shillings paid two-thirds of the year's rent – and with enough land to produce oats and potatoes, and grass to feed a cow for milk, a family could live comfortably.[6] The Burnes family could have had this kind of existence at Alloway. William, however, was more ambitious and leased a farm of 90 acres, although he agreed a rent that was too high. The process of modernising farming required a large investment of cash, time and backbreaking labour. The business was not always well understood, and a hopeful farmer might take on more work and a higher rent than he could manage. A Galloway minister understood the problem: 'Nothing can be more harmful and impolitic to the improvement of agriculture, than the proprietors of land raising it ... to a racked rent in its natural state. This damps the spirit of industrious tenants, [and] throws them into a state of despair.'[7] One of Robert's early poems described the approach of harvest:

Now waving grain, wide o'er the plain,
Delights the weary farmer ...[8]

– but at Mount Oliphant the corn was sparse, and despair was close.

From Mount Oliphant the family moved to Lochlea, ten miles north-east. Robert was by then 18 years old. The new farm was not much different from the old one, the work was similar and equally hard, but it had to be done. As the proverb put it, 'He ne'er did a gude darg [day's work] that gaed grumbling about it'. The world Burns was brought up in depended on the basis of loyalty to the group of people on the farm: they did not want to let one another down. Farming people were beholden to landlords and lawyers whose goals were different, and whose first commitment was to profit. These were the men who rented the sour, unimproved land to William Burnes and left him to overtax his underfed frame. He paid the rent with his health.

Scottish farming was moving out from subsistence into a more productive phase in which the farms fed the growing cities, and farmers and lairds could make thumping profits. The Burnes family found themselves in the middle of this change, labouring to modernise, but without the benefit of the richer crops which were yet to come. They were also vulnerable to bad weather, and a sequence of poor harvests started in 1782.[9] That summer was particularly cold, and as early as 31 October the unripened corn was buried by snow in Stirlingshire. The following years were blighted by long spells of bad weather, and the eruption of a volcano in Iceland cast a fog over western Europe. Twelve miles from the Burnes's farm, John Muir at New Cumnock kept a diary: 'potatoes frosted black' he wrote on 18 August 1784, and he went on to record frost in the middle of June 1785.[10] That autumn the harvest, which usually took a month, was so small that on one Ayrshire farm it was completed in eleven days.[11] Not only was the weather bad, from time to time it was extreme. One Sunday in 1789 was so hot that the minister fainted in the pulpit, and the following winter there was snow and a high wind: 'New Cumnock church was filled with snow from end to end, which was cleared out by the bellman and his wife.'[12]

New farming methods were being introduced in Lowland Scotland.[13] The working horse was a novelty, at first ploughing land which had not yet been improved by liming or draining, like the fields at Mount Oliphant and Lochlea. The light, two-wheeled cart, drawn by one horse, was another innovation, enabling coal and lime to be brought to the farm, and making it easier to spread farmyard manure over the land. The use of the cart depended on better roads. In Burns's time the road system around Lochlea was being recast so that roads went round hills, not over them. While the Burnes were there, John Loudon Macadam, born in Ayr three years before Burns, bought the estate of Sauchrie, south of Alloway. He then started the improvements to roads which became known as 'Macadamisation', involving the use of graded stones to make a firm surface which drained easily. An old woman who disliked the freer flow of traffic said, 'Odds, he'll be pitting the auld country on wheels and whombling it into intae the Atlantic'. Other lairds were improving the appearance and productivity of the countryside by planting trees.

William Burnes died at Lochlea in 1784 and was buried at Alloway. On the day of his funeral, two saddled horses stood facing in the same direction, one in front of the other, poles were hung fore-and-aft between the stirrups, and the coffin was slung between the poles. With the mourners on foot, the plain procession made its way through the fields to Tarbolton, down the long slow descent into Ayr, over the Brig, and then out to Alloway. This was the funeral of a successful teacher, a man who had time to read widely despite being loaded with labour in the fields. For Robert, his best pupil, it was a painful time. He was fearful that Lochlea was not productive enough to feed and clothe the family – he said he was 'half-mad, half-fed, half-sarkit [half-clothed]'.[14]

Later that year Robert and his brother Gilbert moved a couple of miles to another farm in a similar situation. Mossgiel sits on top of a ridge which runs east-west: there is a narrow band of distant hills, bare moors, and a clear sight of the rain clouds as they bear in from the sea, a shifting mist falling on the fields. The farm looks north to Fenwick Moor, south to the higher moorland that leads to Galloway, east to round hills, and from nearby (though not from the farmhouse) west to the Firth of Clyde and Arran's bare serrated ridge. This great expansive view never explicitly emerged in Burns' writing, but was always present as a perspective, a sense of distance, an awareness of other landscapes and lives. As he wrote in 'The Vision':

Here rivers in the sea were lost;
There mountains to the skies were tost:
Here tumbling billows mark'd the coast,
*   With surging foam;*
There, distant shone Art's lofty boast,
*   The lordly dome.*[15]

From Mossgiel Burns could see a dozen parishes or more, a vision of human diversity: people shepherding, fishing, and tilling other kinds of soil. Around this time, 40 or 50 Beltane (1 May) bonfires could be seen at once on these open uplands of Kyle, flaring each community's awareness of supernatural traditions.[16] While he was living at Mossgiel, Burns wrote most of his poems which deal with the supernatural in the restless tumbling sea of creativity along which he was swept in 1785-86: 'Death and Doctor Hornbook', 'Halloween' and the 'Address to the Deil'.

Mauchline was a large village a mile from Mossgiel but invisible from it, set in a hollow, with houses, howffs, and peopled streets on the road from Kilmarnock to Nithsdale. Country women on their way to the Mauchline fairs stopped at the 'drucken [drunken] steps', where there was a ford over a burn on the road near Mossgiel, to put on their stockings.[17] On Sunday the folk talked in the kirkyard before the service, and afterwards escaped from the solemn sermon to be sociable again. The minister, 'Daddy' Auld, attempted to control the behaviour of his flock by exhortation and public criticism in the kirk. One device was the 'stool of repentance' on which those guilty of premarital sex were obliged to sit in front of the congregation during the service. Burns, however, having the status of a farmer rather than an employee, and able to pay a fine, was allowed to stand in his pew to acknowledge his guilt. He had discovered the pleasures of drinking whisky and seducing young women.

Kilmarnock, north of Mossgiel and Mauchline, was the one industrial town in Ayrshire, a growing centre of the textile trade with a population of 7000. When Burns wrote of 'Wabster lads / Blackguardin' frae Kilmarnock'[18], he meant carpet weavers. Other prominent activities were printing calico and dressing sheepskin. It was a place for ambitious men, and gave Burns a more challenging audience for his poetry. Five years before, John Wilson had begun to print books there, and in 1786 he produced almost the first non-theological work from his press, *Poems, chiefly in the Scots Dialect*, known to posterity as Burns's Kilmarnock edition.

Burns spent the winter of 1786-87 in Edinburgh and he had his twenty-eighth birthday there. It was the city where the poet Robert Fergusson, Burns's 'elder brother in the Muse', had lived and died twelve years earlier [see *fig.* 18]. Fergusson's Edinburgh was a warm place

> *Where couthy chiels at e'ening meet*
> *Their bizzing craigs and mous to weet ...* [throats, mouths]

in which talk and drinking, music and eating, were all part of the jostling sociability. This was the city that Burns sought and found. He left the sheep and Ayrshire cows, and became for a few months the urban Burns, a literary lion. He passed his share of the lease of Mossgiel to Gilbert.

Burns stayed first in a room in Baxter's Close, near the top of the Royal Mile. The houses which are still standing today in Lady's Stair's Close and James's Court give some idea of the tall, close-packed buildings which were there in 1786. They rose eight or nine stories high: after heavy snow, there was real danger when it fell from the roofs into the depths of a close.[19] The whole of the steep slope on either side of the High Street was crammed with tenements – shops, workshops and flats of all sizes. This densely-built area was where nine-tenths of the population of Edinburgh lived, in a claustrophobia of sandstone and stench, with a view north to the Firth of Forth or south to the Pentland Hills. People moved from one lodging to another, or out to the country, according to the seasons and their varying needs for space. The tenement stairs were vertical thoroughfares, with coal ascending, ashes being brought down, and quiet corners for gossip.

But the character of Edinburgh was changing. On the far side of the Nor' Loch the New Town was being laid out, the rubble anthill being replaced by dressed stone and large windows, ashlar and astragals. Within Burns's lifetime orchards and fields to the south had been built over, and north of the Royal Mile a new bridge gave access to the New Town whose straight Georgian streets contrasted with the 'hie-heapit' centuries-old wynds down the High Street. The Old Town was cluttered, hidden, noisy, and noisome; the New Town open but controlled, designed with long sight lines so that banks and churches could be respected from a distance. In the Old Town, customers came to talk to tradesmen in their shops; in the New Town, goods were displayed behind window glass.[20]

Edinburgh was suddenly a city of fashion. In 1763 the trade of haberdasher scarcely existed, but now its sub-divisions were there in number – mercers, hatters, linen-drapers, milliners, hosiers, glovers – all the trades that the middle classes needed to make their appearance fashionable. A generation before, servant women wore woollen clothes like their country counterparts: when Burns arrived they had cloaks and silk caps, decorated with ribbons.

Two changes must have been significant to Burns. The first was the rapid development of the book trade, resulting in the possibility of a successful Scots author receiving handsome payments. A woman remembered that in the middle of the century the 'bookseller's shopes were not stuffed as they are now with Novels and Magazines'[21] – nor with poems in the Scots dialect – and by the 1780s reading had become a matter of fashion. Publishing and bookselling had emerged as solid and lucrative forms of commerce, and successful men in the book trade joined other magnates who were to be seen in the High Street. As Robert Fergusson put it:

> Thus bus'ness, weighty bus'ness, comes;
> The trader glowrs, he doubts, he hums.[22]

David Hume, whom we now remember as a philosopher, was said to have been paid £5000 for the second part of his history of Britain; and another historian, William Robertson, received £4500 for one of his works. Burns did not reach this level of opulence, but he did make a profit of about £800 on the Edinburgh edition of his poems (1787) [see fig. 16]. (When he joined the excise service, his salary was £50 a year.)

The second change was that the stool of repentance was no longer used in Edinburgh.[23]

Edinburgh had ceased to be a seat of government, but it was the home of the Scottish legal system, and as the place where the General Assembly of the Church of Scotland met it was the ecclesiastical centre. For the week of the Assembly the city thronged with ministers and elders. A wit imagined the provisioning of such a gathering sucking in food from the Firth of Forth:

> The Forth was plunder'd of its fish,
> That they might have a dainty dish;
> Salmon, cod and cabelow, [salt cod]
> Into their bellies they did stow,

> *At oysters too they did not bogle,* [i.e. boggle]
> *Which made them at our ladies ogle.*[24]

Burns was elected a member of two of the city's clubs. The Royal Company of Archers was emerging from a couple of generations of disgrace, caused by prominent members having been Jacobites. Half a century earlier the poet Allan Ramsay had been an Archer and praised the Company in verse: perhaps the members hoped that Burns would be a second laureate. More likely, however, he was drawn into both clubs by his masonic connections. The membership of the Royal Caledonian Hunt Club was made up of noblemen and wealthy commoners, and Robert Burns. The other creative figure who often appears in their minute books was Nathaniel Gow, the fiddler who performed at each of the Club's annual meetings. Gow was a paid employee, but Burns was a member. The Club gave Burns its patronage – £25 for 100 copies of the Edinburgh edition of his poems (1787) – and one imagines that some individual Hunters patronised him too.

Burns had been brought up with a distant view of the Highlands, but in Edinburgh he met Gaels in greater number than before. The town guard – 'black banditti' according to Fergusson – were mostly ex-soldiers from the north. There were Highland lairds and their families, particularly in winter, living on the rents from their estates. The Disarming Act, which had been passed after the Battle of Culloden, banning the wearing of Highland dress in the Highlands, was repealed in 1782. In the Lowlands, Highland identity was beginning to be enjoyed, and there was a craze for *Ossian* (1765), the Celtic epic written by James Macpherson. Burns already saw himself as 'the Scottish bard', and his interest in Celtic culture enabled him to feel that he was representing the whole country. It may also have strengthened his Jacobitism, although his natural sympathy was for anyone, mouse or exiled monarch, who had been treated unfairly. Nonetheless, at the end of his first stay in Edinburgh, Burns made a tour of the Highlands, going as far as Inverness.

Robert and his family moved to Nithsdale in 1788, farming at Ellisland, and the following year he started his career as an exciseman [*fig. 26*]. He was from this point committed to Jean Armour, and the children she had borne him and would in the future bear, the last on the day of his funeral. Nithsdale was broader than the Ayrshire valleys, framed by bigger hills. Upper Nithsdale was, according to a contemporary, a desolate country, where the trees were ragged and withered.[25] In contrast, parts of lower Nithsdale were 'covered with different sorts of trees, which greatly adds to the beauty of the country'.[26] One of the local lairds was the Duke of Queensberry, 'Old Q', known as the rake of Piccadilly, who paid for his fun in London by selling mature timber in Dumfriesshire. Henry Mackenzie, the first major Edinburgh figure to praise Burns, imagined the River Nith complaining:

> *The worm that gnaw'd my bonie trees,*
> *That reptile wears a ducal crown.*[27]

Nithsdale is the north-east edge of the round, lonely Galloway hills where farming was mostly the grazing of sheep on coarse grass. March dykes – boundary walls – were being built over the hills, revealing the control that lairds had over the open land.[28]

Burns was familiar with the landscape because he rode through it, carrying out his new duties as an exciseman.[29] The exciseman was not popular: he was a tax-collector by another name. Ten years after Burns died another poet wrote this scathing epitaph:

> *For now, he's left time's fleeting stage,*
> *Wha pit the Ale-wives in a rage,*
> *Nae mair their bowies will he gage,* [barrels]
> *Wi' his foull stick.*[30]

Part of the exciseman's income came from a share of the proceeds of the auction of any contraband he found. He was the visible part of government, with powers of entry and search, encouraged to use different routes each week to surprise the people he visited. In Upper Nithsdale Burns's calls included two tanners (to be visited three times a week), eleven maltsters (to be called upon five times a fortnight), three wine sellers, 21 spirit dealers, 27 tobacco dealers and 15 tea merchants. He also monitored the stocks held by spirit dealers in an attempt to detect smuggling – which might mean local illicit distilling as well as the importation of contraband. It was a highly administrative job, as this complaint to his neighbour Maria Riddell about the paperwork suggests:

> *Fine employment for a poet's pen! There is a species of Human genius that I call the Gin-horse Class: what enviable dogs they are!*

> *Round, & round, & round they go ... without an idea or wish*
> *beyond their circle; fat, sleek, stupid, patient, quiet & contented.*[31]

Burns saw these men as natural employees of the Excise Commissioners.

As an exciseman, Burns assessed the tax which was due. The money was received by his colleague, the Collector. Collectors were told not to ride 'between dusk and dawn'. [See *fig. 25*].

Most posts in the Excise were filled through patronage, and some excisemen in Scotland were English. This brought an acute awareness of status and the importance of aristocratic contacts. Excisemen often thought themselves socially superior to farmers and tradesmen, and this made them awkward members of country society.

The case of Mungo Campbell illustrates the social ambiguity of the exciseman.[32] He was the son of the provost of Ayr, but had served in the ranks in the Scots Greys for twelve years rather than having been an officer. Having left the Army, he went into the Highlands with the Earl of Loudon at the time of the Jacobite rebellion in 1745/46, and was rewarded for his loyalty to the Crown by being given a post in the Excise. He seems to have believed that either his social standing or his professional position gave him the right to poach, and when the Earl of Eglinton challenged him he shot the nobleman dead. His action implied that he thought himself as good as a laird. By committing suicide before his execution, he placed himself in a smaller and more extreme category of outsider.

While at Ellisland, Burns wrote 'Tam o' Shanter', about an encounter between a man and 'the hellish legion' of witches. It has been said that superstition was less important to Burns than, later, to Walter Scott, James Hogg or Robert Louis Stevenson. They regarded it as something different from the day-to-day world, a source of terror. To Burns it was something which his neighbours believed affected the daily life on the farm, and was in a sense natural, or at least unremarkable.

The move to Nithsdale made Burns into what was beginning to be called a crofter: a man with land to farm plus other work which brought in a steady income. For him, it was not a success. 'This farm has undone my enjoyment of myself,' he wrote to his brother Gilbert. 'It is a ruinous affair on all hands – But let it go to hell!'[33] When Burns wrote a description of the lending library he had helped to set up in Dunscore parish, he ended by saying that 'a peasant who can read, and enjoy such books, is certainly a much superior being to his neighbour who, perhaps, stalks beside his team, very little removed, except in shape, from the beasts he drives'.[34] He seems to have been declaring that he had had enough of the countryside and country people: he wanted the more stimulating life of the town.

Burns moved into Dumfries in November 1791, where he was to live for the last four and a half years of his life. The family's leaving of the land was part of the fall of the population in the countryside and the growth of urban centres. In towns the government and its bureaucratic arms were visible as they were not in the countryside, through institutions like the Post Office. Dumfries inns had names that supported the status quo: for example 'The George', 'The King's Arms' and 'The Coach and Horses' (suggesting the Royal Mail).[35] Local government was conspicuous in the form of the tolbooth which stood, like the one at Ayr, in the middle of the High Street, attracting attention by blocking the way. Single-storied Ellisland was limewashed white: Dumfries was built of earthy red-brown sandstone, often two stories high. The streets, drawing-rooms and taverns of Dumfries formed a larger stage than Mauchline for Burns to play the parts of poet, songwriter, exciseman and local figure.

By the spring of 1796 he was ill, and beyond the reach of any kind of help [see *fig.* 17]. Modern medical opinion says that his heart, weakened by rheumatic fever, was about to give out. His last attempt at a cure was to visit the healing well at Brow, on the Solway Coast. On 21 July the thread of life was nicked; his breath was choked. He was buried in St Michael's kirkyard as the Royal Dumfries Volunteers fired three volleys, and the band of the Cinque Ports Fencibles played the dead march from Handel's oratorio 'Saul'. This was not as incongruous as it sounds: Burns's songs had already been set to music by Haydn and Beethoven.

The great Burns scholar David Daiches summed up the bard's achievement:

> *He created a glorious Indian Summer for native Scottish literature and in doing so made himself known to peoples and to generations far removed from both the heady air of his disintegrating century and the split personality of his history-racked country.*[36]

NOTES

1   The basis for this chapter is Mackay (1992).
2   *Ibid.*, p. 61.
3   Banks (1939).
4   Chambers (1858), p. 324.
5   *Old Statistical Account*: Dalrymple.
6   *OSA*: Ballantrae.
7   *OSA*: Tongland.
8   Robertson (1904), p. 357; Kinsley (1968), p. 5. The quotations from the work of Robert Burns used in this publication are from J. Logie Robertson's edition, and reference is also given to James Kinsley's scholarly edition.
9   Lamb (1982), p. 236.
10 Steven (1899), pp. 39, 40.
11 *Ibid.*, p. 40.
12 *Ibid.*, p. 34.
13 Fenton (2000).
14 Robertson (1904), p. 52; Kinsley (1968), p. 103.
15 *Ibid.* (1904), p. 53; (1968), p. 105.
16 Aiton (1811), pp. 153-54.
17 Marked on the Ordnance Survey six-inch map, Ayrshire Sheet 28 (1859).
18 Robertson (1904), p. 33; Kinsley (1968), p. 131.
19 *Scots Magazine*, 44 (1782), p. 162.
20 Creech (1791), pp. 63-93.
21 Mure (1854), p. 269.
22 Fergusson (1807), p. 342.
23 *Scots Magazine*, 45 (1783), pp. 617-23.
24 'Claudero' (1771), p. 13.
25 Heron (1799), pp. 58-59.
26 *OSA*: Kirkmahoe.
27 Ewing (1919).
28 Naismith (1795).
29 Smith (1989).
30 Cock (1806), p. 33.
31 Ferguson and Roy (1985), vol. 2, p. 217.
32 Robertson (1908), vol. 2, pp. 109-12.
33 Ferguson and Roy (1985), p. 1.
34 *OSA*: Dunscore.
35 Mackay (1992), p. 484.
36 Daiches (1966), p. 320.

CHAPTER 2

The People
of Lowland Scotland

ROBERT Burns lived on the edge of Europe. Ten thousand years
earlier, the glaciers of the Ice Age had ground Ayrshire's rocks into
a clay soil. This was the physical context in which he grew up. What
made up the cultural world in which Burns was raised and lived?

Culture has a very broad meaning including language, beliefs, customs, objects and the many forms of art. A substantial part of Scottish
culture was based on the languages used in Scotland – Scots and English.
Scots is a Germanic tongue which landed in Britain in the sixth century
with the Angles, and which in the twelfth century became one of the
languages of Lowland Scotland. The first extensive written work in
Scots was John Barbour's 'Brus', composed in the 1370s, a long poem
about Robert Bruce and the wars of independence. English moved to
centre stage when in 1560 the Scottish Protestant reformers adopted the
English translation of the Bible made in Geneva. In 1611 it was replaced
by the solemn cadences of the King James Bible.

In the second half of the eighteenth century, people in the Lowlands
spoke Scots, read English in books and newspapers, and wrote in a
mixture – or mixter-maxter – of the two. Most of Burns's best verse is in
Scots, although all but one of his letters is written in English; and in 'Tam
o' Shanter' he uses both languages so that the story is told in different
voices. Scots had already accepted words from other languages. In 'The
Twa Dogs', Luath's 'Honest, sonsie, baws'nt face' uses a word from

Gaelic, *sonas*, meaning good fortune; another comes from Old French, *bawsent,* meaning black with a white stripe. When Burns addresses the mouse whose nest he had destroyed, he sympathises with the fact that because it is December the creature has no materials for another, 'an nae-thin, now, to big a new one'. *Big* is from the Norse. In 'Tam o' Shanter' too, Burns describes his main character as 'a skellum, a blethering, blustering, drunken blellum', *skellum* having come from the Dutch word for a rascal.

One of the characteristics of Burns's poems and songs is his use of exact, economical language. This he learned from ballads, the Bible and proverbs. Ballads and proverbs also provided psychological insight, and the Bible set out stories which enabled thinking about power and responsibility in real human situations.

Alexander Johnston, a minister in Aberdeenshire, at the end of the eighteenth century pointed to three ways in which language had been used: the proverb, the friet or superstition, and the song.[1] He said that all were now in the past (not true, although their use was in decline), and he claimed that they had been replaced by the values of the 'sinical Chesterfield' – the values set out in the *Letters* (1774) of the cynical Earl of Chesterfield, which detailed an approach to life based on self-interest. Johnston was regretting the passing of a way of life based on loyalty to the community, as well as the departure of some forms of creativity which were in the hands of the people.

The minister saw proverbs as a guide to the transaction of daily life, calling them 'the laws of propriety and prudence'. They were pieces of practical psychology: 'Danger past, God forgotten.'[2] They sometimes showed a black humour: the modern saying 'You can't take it with you' was expressed as 'There's nae poackits [pockets] in a shroud'. They formed a framework for dealing with the world, formulae to be drawn upon whenever suitable, containing a blunt eloquence, combined with a tough-minded way of thinking: 'A fool uttereth all his mind', 'The words of the wise are as goads', or the biblical 'Curse God, and die'.

There were also familiar statements of value, with which people made judgements on their neighbours, the state of the world, and the work of God. These were, like the proverb, a way of assessing a person or their behaviour. The Bible said, 'Consider the lilies of the field: they toil not, neither do they spin, yet Solomon in all his glory was not arrayed like one of these'. It could be applied to anyone who was well dressed. A secular condemnation of ignorance was, 'He doesna ken a B from a bull's fit [foot]'. Burns used this terse manner to assess the society in which he lived ('The rank is but the guinea's stamp, The man's the gowd for a' that'). Other familiar sayings provided irony: 'He's a hardy man to draw a sword at a haggis', 'He's as bold as a Lammermuir lion' (meaning a sheep), 'You may ding the Deil [beat the Devil] into a wife, but you'll never ding him out of her'. Burns was certainly no stranger to irony.

The friet was a belief 'enforcing the duty to the neighbour or friend, contained in the code of vulgar good-breeding'. In other words, it encouraged sensible behaviour, by producing a social pressure or public awareness of what ought to be done in specific circumstances. For example, it was thought unlucky for a woman who had just borne a child to be visited by her neighbours until she had been 'churched', that is taken to church to give thanks to God for a safe delivery. This emphasised the importance of thanking God, explained Johnston. Once she had been churched, however, the arrival of every visitor was customarily met with lots of food; the point being to feed the new mother to build up her strength. It was also said that the dead were disturbed if a tear were to fall on the winding sheet: in Johnston's words this was intended to control behaviour, to prevent 'wild or frantic sorrow'. People believed that misfortune would follow if a cat were to jump over a corpse: this was to stop carnivorous animals from preying on the dead. Burns himself observed this kind of tradition. In one instance he asked a servant to carry a Bible and a bowl of salt as the first person to enter the new farmhouse at Ellisland. Salt had once been costly, and there was something magical in its ability to preserve meat.

Mr Johnston's final category was song, which he described as 'a flattering chronicle' of history and thus a way of creating and sustaining identity. The kind of song he had in mind was a proud description of heroism. It might celebrate Border reivers like Johnnie Armstrong or Kinmont Willie, or battles like Harlaw (1411) and the most significant one fought in Ayrshire, at Largs (1263), where the Scots defeated the Vikings and broke their hold on the Western Isles. The latter was described in 'Hardyknute':

> *In thrawis of death with wallowit cheik,* [withered]
> *All panting on the plain,*
> *The fainting corps of warriors lay*
> *Neir to arise again.*[3]

The best songs were like this, swift tales of loyalty and treachery in a stripped-down language with the directness of a country and western song. Johnston contrasted these noble ballads with the fashionable music of his time, 'to my sorrow, no longer painting the character of antient times, [they] may vie in inanity with the ordinary vehicles of Italian music'.

The big epic ballads dealt with large emotional themes: they were an education in human psychology. They described cruelty, anger and selfishness, sometimes self-sacrifice, and perhaps at the end offered forgiveness and hope. Robert Heron, Burns's first biographer, named some ballads which were popular in south-west Scotland, such as 'Love Gregory' in which a pregnant woman whose lover has gone to sea is disowned by both her own family and his.[4] The ballad poses questions which are at the same time both emotional and practical: what does she do, and what happens when the man reappears?[5] Another favourite was 'Young Beichan', in which a man soldiering in a Mohammedan land falls in love with his captor's daughter. When he is released she follows him to England, finds him, and converts to Christianity so they can be married. It is about the thrill of the exotic, and the power of love to bridge cultures.[6] Ballads were not only performed on a special occasion, but were rather an evening staple, and people imagined them while sewing, sowing, washing and threshing. Nor were they works of art to be received with silent respect; like soap operas they were stories about life, and the hearers talked about the motivations and pains which they set out.

In pious Scotland, education at home was a matter of repeating psalms and long catechisms which worked doctrine into the young mind. This is where the Burnes family was exceptional, with a widely-read father talking and reading to his children, and encouraging them when they explored books far beyond dogmatic theology. Alexander Carse, the artist, was eleven years younger than Burns, and in a painting produced in 1795 he showed himself and his sister listening to their mother reading the Bible [see *fig.* 21]. It is a picture of serious thoughts, and one imagines that the atmosphere at Lochlea was similar.

The most common printed book was the Bible. It was the basis for the Kirk's teaching, and also a part of popular culture. Place names were chosen from it, such as Pisgah (from which Moses saw the Promised Land) on the hill above Prestwick, and also near Maybole. As in every Christian country, forenames were chosen from the Scriptures. The characters in the Bible were treated as part of the local community and known by familiar names such as 'Edie' for Adam. The blind John Milton, whose 'Paradise Lost' was read as an extension of the Book of Genesis, was 'Blin Jock',[7] and there was so much interest in his epic poem that it was one of the first books printed at Kilmarnock (1785) and Ayr (1791). Daily conversation was peppered with quotations from the Bible. We can get an impression of this in a letter which Burns wrote when he moved to Ellisland: 'I have taken a Farm on the banks of the Nith, and, in imitation of the old Patriarchs get Man-servants and Maid-servants, and flocks and herds, and beget Sons and Daughters.'[8] And Burns's 'The Patriarch', about Jacob and his wives, is in the tradition of turning characters from the Scriptures into more rounded individuals with full lives, and laughing at their human predicaments.[9] In a similarly friendly spirit, John Mayne described one of the floral decorations at the procession before the shooting for the Siller Gun at Dumfries in 1777:

> *Amang the flow'ry forms they weave,*
> *There's* Adam *to the life, and* Eve:
> *She, wi' the apple in her neeve,* [fist]
>   *Enticing* Adam;
> *While* Satan's *laughing in his sleeve*
>   *At him and madam!*[10]

The New Testament also featured in daily life. In Scotland in the seventeenth and eighteenth centuries, people believed that the apostle Andrew had been made a saint as a reward for having given Christ the oatcake which ended his fast for forty days and forty nights. There was a prejudice against working with an iron implement on Good Friday, the day of the Crucifixion, because Christ was crucified with iron nails. The smith was expected to abstain from work, and his wife not to wear her apron (the nails were often carried in a smith's wife's apron).[11]

    The Kirk stressed the word of God, as set out in the Bible, as the basis for all faith, and so a knowledge of the scriptures was valued. However, the Bible also raised many starting points for debate. This is what Burns is talking about when he describes Francis Grose's making of antiquarian conjectures with little information to start from:

> *Forbye, he'll shape you aff fu' gleg* [quickly]
> *The cut of Adam's philibeg;* [kilt]

The knife that nicket Abel's craig — [throat]
 He'll prove you fully
It was a faulding jockteleg, [pocket knife]
 Or lang-kail gullie.[12] [large knife]

The dominant doctrinal position in the Kirk was held by the 'Auld Lichts'. They believed in the real, lurid existence of Hell, and that rigid rules of behaviour had been set out in the Bible. All this was of the most intense interest, and one minister commented that 'the vulgar read almost nothing but books on religious subjects'. This caused the attendant problem of people being overfond of controversial theological books. It was the role of the clergyman 'to recommend books of a more rational and instructive nature'.[13] Another man said that the reform of farming methods would be established more quickly if farmers did not waste their time arguing about religion. The 'Auld Lichts' were so-called to distinguish them from the 'New Lichts' like Burns who thought that human conduct should be evaluated in human terms, looking at the individual's intentions and the effects one's actions had on others.

The supernatural was part of the emotional cosmos of the eighteenth century. William Aiton, a lawyer, said that in the 1770s most people in Ayrshire still believed in wraiths, ghosts, witches and omens – and he criticised ministers for indulging themselves in theological controversies rather than attacking widespread superstitions.[14] George Campbell followed Burns's example by publishing his poems at Kilmarnock in 1787: his version of 'The Cotter's Saturday Night' had songs of love and murder in the middle of the evening, and the night ended with fairy and ghost stories.[15]

In trying to understand what people thought in Burns's time, the supernatural – that is, a world or set of worlds beyond the one that we live in from hour to hour, and in which various beings live and act – can be seen as separate from superstition. Superstitious beliefs are not usually linked with one another and have diverse origins. One source, which we have already met, is the survival of past values such as salt being rare and costly. Another is sympathetic magic, a very old idea, based on the notion that one thing can be used to affect another because the two can be seen as being linked by their shape or some other quality. One treatment for toothache, for example, was to carry the jaw of a hedgehog in a waistcoat pocket: the animal's bone was in some sort of contact with the human one, and its spines represented pain and drew away the ache. National Museums Scotland preserves a goose's throat with lead shot in it, from Balmaghie, worn round the neck to prevent whooping-cough: the link is between different kinds of congestion in different kinds of throats.[16] One suspects that this specific piece of sympathetic magic had emerged in the eighteenth century, when a lead shot mill was in operation at Creetown.[17] If someone setting out on a journey found a knife on the open road, few would dare to lift it because its sharp edge threatened the purpose of the journey which was being made: the journey was imagined as something vulnerable which was open to being damaged.[18]

To counter this tendency, learned men were proud of the ability to produce rational explanations of strange events. When James Melville, an east coast minister who had helped shipwrecked sailors from the Spanish armada, observed an eclipse of the Sun in 1598, he called it an 'amazfull, vglie, alriche [eldritch] darkness', in which he admitted that he fell to his knees. He had had an intense emotional experience, and part of his response was rational. He wrote a sonnet to declare that the eclipse was caused by the Moon coming between the Sun and the Earth. Nevertheless, he still regarded it as a sign of an evil influence coming between Christ and the Kirk, and thought himself justified when four leading ministers died the following year.[19] Even the learned could believe that something frightening in the behaviour of the cosmos could have unhappy effects in Scotland.

Another world paralleled the supernatural, that of the living history which was sung about and discussed, particularly events which had taken place nearby. It was as real as the supernatural, and equally invisible. One of the first books to take hold of Burns's imagination was Blind Harry's life of William Wallace. The Wallace family had lands in Ayrshire in the Middle Ages, and one of the reasons why Burns valued the friendship and advice of Frances Anna Dunlop, to whom he wrote many letters, was that she had Wallace blood. Places as well as people act as the holders of memories: the patriotic young poet visited Wallace's hiding place in Leglen Wood on the River Ayr in 1786. Robert Bruce had been born at Turnberry, and christened at Crossraguel Abbey. The font was moved the couple of miles to Kirkoswald where it is still in the kirkyard opposite the schoolroom where Burns learned land surveying [see *fig. 9*].

There were also many remnants of the medieval church in the area. Kirk Alloway, barely 500 yards from the Burnes's house, was built in

1516. There is still a stone bowl outside the church for holy water. The Auld Kirk in Ayr, where Burns worshipped as a boy, was on the site of a medieval Franciscan friary. North of Ayr is St Nicholas at Prestwick, another little church on a knoll looking out on Ayr Bay. There was also the shattered magnificence of Crossraguel Abbey.

How was knowledge spread through the community? Most people could read: the Kirk had created an educational system with a school in every parish so that each individual could have a personal familiarity with the Bible. Printed material was passed around, and read aloud: one reason why eighteenth-century newspapers are now rare is that most copies were read to pieces, having been handed from household to household. Newspapers ensured that people knew what was going on in imperial politics and world events.

Much practical knowledge was held by the people as a whole, shared and discussed, including an intense familiarity with the locality: which fields drained well, where herbs were to be found, where the minister paused on his afternoon walk. Some forms of knowledge were held by individuals on behalf of the community. Often elderly people were the repositories of information about health and disease, and women tended to be the ones who knew traditional songs and stories. In contrast, some specialists like professionals and tradesmen had knowledge which gave them a distinctive language. Knowledge is power. As the eighteenth century progressed, more and more men regarded knowledge as a property they could hold and use to their financial advantage and to achieve status. In towns, the trade guilds were a system for preventing the spread of knowledge; although technically torpid, they were shrewd and held a lucrative position until the growth of industry made them irrelevant.

The most widely distributed forms of printed material were broadsheets and chapbooks.[20] Broadsheets were single sheets of type printed on one side, often with a simple woodblock illustration near the top. They were produced at short notice to provide details of some disaster or other surprising event – the fact that something had happened would already have been told by word of mouth – or to give the words of a new topical song. In Burns's time chapbooks were becoming more common, pamphlets of four or eight pages, and sometimes more, easy for travelling merchants to carry in quantity, and containing the same kind of material as a broadsheet. He wrote of 'Excellent New Songs that are hawked about the country in baskets, or exposed in stalls in the street'.[21]

The chapbook and broadsheet were replaced in the nineteenth century by cheap weekly newspapers, each copy of which carried a far wider range of material, and included a new and exciting form of printed communication – advertising.

By the eighteenth century south-west Scotland was not isolated, and the people there had a good knowledge of what was happening in Edinburgh, London and the rest of the world. Newspapers from Glasgow, Edinburgh and London, although expensive, reached lairds and ministers and, through them, other members of the community. At Ellisland, Burns thanked the neighbouring landlord Robert Riddell for enabling him to know:

> How the collieshangie works [noisy dispute]
> Atween the Russians and the Turks.[22]

Dumfries was one of the first provincial towns in Scotland to have a weekly paper, established in 1777. At fairs people talked to cattle dealers who toured the country. Travellers like Dr Samuel Johnson came and saw, and lawyers like his friend James Boswell of Auchinleck practised in London before retiring to their Ayrshire estates. Boswell was a link between Ayrshire and the intellectual side of London. Another was the minister of Auchinleck, married to the sister of Colen Campbell, the fashionable architect who had great success in the 1720s. In the second half of the eighteenth century it became usual for landed families to spend the winter in Edinburgh and the summer on their estates. Both they and their servants brought the city's knowledge and attitudes to the country.

If words were one aspect of Scottish culture, another was the selection of objects with which people surrounded themselves, the plenishing of the house, the choice of objects for work and for display, and so on. When Burns wrote to his friend James Smith in Mauchline that 'Some rhyme a neebor's name to lash',[23] he probably had in mind the attack made in verse by Saunders Tait upon William Burnes. It concerned Burnes's dispute with his landlord David McClure over the lease on Lochlea. McClure had, as was usual, made a loan to Burnes when he took possession of the farm to enable him to stock it.

> The horse, corn, pets, kail, kye and lures,
> Cheese, pease, beans, rye, wool, house and flours,

> Pots, pans, crans, tongs, brace-spits and skeurs,
>   The milk and barm,
> Each thing they had was a' McLure's,
>   He stock'd the farm.[24]

Tait makes it sound as though McClure had given all these things, but Burnes had paid for them, and had the debt as well as the stock and the hardware. Alongside purchases like these, many things were made on the farm.

The material world in which Burns lived was centered on the intense use of local resources.[25] Basketwork came from the willow, reeds and long grasses which grew in damp ground. Wood had been rare, and used sparingly. English travellers saw Scotland as a country bald of trees. When Burns described the River Ayr – 'Auld hermit Ayr staw [stole] thro' his woods'[26] – he was drawing attention to the mature hardwood in the river's gorge, in such contrast to the limited number of trees around the open fields. Timber was used where it was essential, for the couples of the roof, and not for flooring where the bare earth was covered with rushes. Food on a farm was largely the produce of that farm, particularly in an area like Ayrshire where dairying was well established. Houses were made from earth, or from local stones at first left by glaciation, or lifted from the fields, and then from nearby quarries. Materials for thatching were to be found by every burn. Even luxury objects were made from simple materials, like Burns's bone toddy ladles and an inkwell that Burns gave John Lapraik in 1793, formed from a pony's hoof. Both of these are displayed in the Burns House, Dumfries.

Cloth was made from sheep's wool and the patches of flax that the farmer grew to make his own linen. Women made and bleached their own linen and spun their own wool, then the role of the weaver was to make the cloth for them, not for the wider market. Finally, the women of the farm cut and stitched it to make clothes for the family. Men and women in the Lowlands, Burns included, wore a woollen plaid which could go over the shoulders or the head, and did not require the skill of the tailor. Clothes were worn for years, and when a piece of clothing had worn to the point of uselessness, it was broken down into the fibres and a new yarn spun. Even a laird wore old shirts with new collars stitched in.

Clothes were important, for some almost their only personal possession. The first essential for a family was to feed itself over the whole year; but once food was assured people wanted to dress as well as they could manage. A proverb said, 'If it werena for the belly, the back wad wear gowd', and when courting, men gave women presents of pieces of things to wear such as a pair of shoes or stockings. Fergusson's poem 'Braid Claith' warned male suitors what would happen if they did not dress with care:

> For, gin he come wi' coat thread-bare,
> A feg for him she winna care,
> But crook her bonny mou' fu' sair, [mouth]
>   And scald him baith.
> Lovers should aye their travel spare
>   Without Braid Claith.[27]

Towards the end of the eighteenth century the wages paid in cash to servants increased and young women were able to buy factory-made cotton cloth so they could 'busk fu' braw' in search of a partner. At the beginning of 'Tam o' Shanter', Burns wrote of 'chapman billies'. The chapman, travelling to farms and fairs, selling cloth, dyes, ribbons and other haberdashery, was an agent of change, and his goods an indicator of it. Burns himself wore the typical farmer's coat of blue, dyed with the imported plant indigo which was cheap, reliable and produced a colour that did not fade. For special occasions he had more exotic clothing, of which there is one tantalising survival, a beautiful set of spherical agate buttons [see *fig*. 28]: what colour of coat or waistcoat were they for? For a specific situation, the masonic meeting, Burns used the apron given to him by a fellow mason. It was a display of symbols, something like a banner, but to be worn on the person rather than carried on a pole.

South-west Scotland had long-standing links with Europe and America [see *fig*. 15]. In one issue of the *Dumfries Weekly Journal* in 1788, local merchants advertised that they had for sale a selection of imported grass seed, Memel timber, Riga wainscot, Swedish iron and deals, Archangel deals, battens and tar; wine, tea, oils, dyestuffs, bitter oranges for making marmalade, and sugar from the West Indies.[28] And increasingly manufactured goods came from the great centres of Birmingham and London. Burns had a pair of flint pistols made by David Blair [see *fig*. 25], and his Excise carbine was by Owen Probin. Both of these gunmakers worked in Birmingham.

A central theme of this book is that Scotland was changing rapidly during Burns's lifetime. More and better roads, and larger numbers of horses, meant that it was easier to get around or borrow a mount if one wanted to ride from Mauchline to Edinburgh, as Burns did when he made his first visit to the capital. For country folk the social world was no longer the fermtoun, where six or ten families worked and lived together, but the smaller group on the farm, where the farmer employed and deployed his servants, and the larger society of village and parish. People were moving to cities, towns and villages, and the population of the countryside was falling. It was easier, too for the mind to move, away from the old certainties of Auld Licht Calvinism towards a kinder and more flexible creed.

Numbering and measuring were also increasingly part of country life. The village of Douglas in Lanarkshire was given a church clock by Mary Queen of Scots in 1565, but such clocks were then rarities. Mauchline had one by 1674 and German clocks with wooden movements were widespread in farmhouses by the end of the eighteenth century. William Burnes had a pocket watch, which passed to Robert after his father's death. Payment in cash increasingly replaced barter and payment in kind: the era of the ledger and double-entry bookkeeping had begun. Professional measurers appeared – land surveyors and excisemen – all counting, weighing and calculating.

In public, people defined their roles by social signs which showed who they were. Farmers were known by their blue coats and long boots. The number of tradesmen increased in the eighteenth century, in town and village, and each trade had its distinctive tools, dress and language. The tools remained after death as symbols on a man's headstone, an anvil for the smith or a loaf for the baker [see *fig.* 27]. The state became visible from day to day through symbolic objects, like the crowned lion door knocker from the Excise Office in Dumfries which is preserved in the Robert Burns Centre. The military volunteer movement was stimulated in the 1790s by the fear of French invasion, bringing not just uniforms but also insignia on items of sociability, such as the arms on the drinking glass of the Royal Dumfries Volunteers. The gentry had been used to placing marks of ownership and status on their possessions – now a larger number of people were doing the same. At the same time more lists were being compiled and becoming increasingly public, like the publishing of births and deaths in the newspapers and all the government record-keeping necessary to raise the taxes which paid for the war. Symbols and lists created visible structures for society, and kept the supernatural in the shadows, shadows which were diminishing as the light of reason and progress shone into more corners of the landscape and the mind.

Farming, by far the largest industry in Scotland, was also subject to rapid change. We have already seen how agricultural improvement affected the Burns family. In the 1770s some farms near Dumfries, at Cargen, were sold: they were advertised as having fields laid out 'in the most regular and commodious manner', fenced with thorn hedges, drystane dykes, and ditches, and sheltered by broad belts of thriving trees.[29] This was an exaggeration, but tree planting had at least started. The work of bringing the land under control was progressing, although there is no evidence of liming or otherwise making the soil more productive. In this period, however, most land was sold or leased on the basis that it was suitable for improvement, not that the work had begun. Twenty years later a great deal had been done. In Kirkmahoe, the parish over the Nith from Ellisland, there had been only two carts in 1750, used for the supply of water; but, another 20 years on, and even the smallest farmer had a cart, and some had several. They carried manure from the steading, and lime from the kiln to the fields; and they brought hawthorns to the farm for hedging, and sandstone for rebuilding the steading. They also enabled the farmer to reach Dumfries to sell corn and vegetables, and to spend his cash with agricultural merchants, provision dealers and drapers.[30]

In the 1780s, at Kelton Hill fair, 15 miles west of Dumfries, two young farmers appeared:

> *Now up an' doun throughout the fair,*
> *They crack'd their eel-skin lashes;*
> *An' gaily show'd their raploch gear,*
> *An', bridles made o' rashes.*[31]

… that is, home-made horse whips, clothes made of raploch, a coarse woollen cloth, and bridles made from rushes gathered in the fields. In contrast, the same poet saw 'Tunbridge toys' for sale, decorated wooden objects at least nominally made in the south of England.

Scotland was being altered, too, by contact with English people, particularly merchants and men who brought their technical skills north of the Border. The most important professions, the kirk and the law, were largely immune from southern entrants because they required a Scottish education. But industrial development in Scotland was driven by new machinery which had been invented in England for making textiles, and the light ploughs which were to transform Scottish farming had their origin in the Rotherham plough. Other influences were more local. Galloway, for example, was close to England; while the counties of Dumfries and Cumberland met along the River Sark. For hundreds, if not thousands of years, there had been trade across the Solway Firth, and now it was growing. This assisted agricultural change through imports of lime and easy access to markets in the towns on the Cumbrian coast. Some changes were even more specific. In the area around Dumfries, wooden clogs, introduced from England, were made and worn. They were formed with a leather upper nailed on to the sole, and 'shod', usually heel and toe, by the blacksmith. It was said that 'they keep the feet remarkably warm and comfortable, and entirely exclude all damp, and thence are thought to contribute highly to the healthiness of the labouring part of the community'.[32]

The countryside had been populated by familiar animals with friendly names, like the Jenny wren, Jenny heron, Nanny Washtail (pied wagtail), and Reid Rab (the robin). The Scots word for a hare is *maukin*, from Matilda. Now, however, the world was being formally listed and catalogued and sometimes sold too. For example, a dealer in Edinburgh offered dozens of varieties of vegetables for the kitchen garden and hothouse. At the same time, competition was becoming more evident and more explicit. In 1792 the Glasgow Florists gave their first prize for pinks to a gardener, the second to a weaver, and the two prizes of the Paisley Society of Florists were also won by weavers. Prizes gave a man local fame, and a book of poems might do so too.

It had always been possible for men of talent and energy to rise in the world. One whose name was well-known in Dumfries was John Hutton, who started as an episcopal minister's herd boy. The minister educated him, and Hutton in time became physician to William of Orange and Queen Mary. He gave his library to the presbytery of Dumfries. By the second half of the eighteenth century opportunities were increasing in number and variety, and Burns understood this. He founded the Batchelors' Club at Tarbolton to give himself and other forward-looking young men experience in public speaking. He became a freemason because it was a sociable way of meeting people of higher social standing, and the success of this tactic was proved when he was in Edinburgh [see *figs* 22, 23, 31]. Joining the Excise and the Royal Dumfries Volunteers also enabled him to widen his circle of contacts.

In contrast to the new-fangled ways, Tam o' Shanter, a resolutely old-fashioned farmer, rode from Ayr to Alloway:

Whiles holding fast his gude blue bonnet;
Whiles crooning o'er some auld Scots sonnet;
Whiles glow'ring round wi' prudent cares,
Lest bogles catch him unawares.[33]

He was wearing traditional clothes, and making himself feel safe by singing a long-familiar ballad. And, at the same time, he was fully alive to the supernatural. Much of Scotland, indeed, still lived in the traditional ways. It was conventional to fear the mischief of witches, and to expect to meet the Devil on the road or in the fields. And here he is!

NOTES

1 *Old Statistical Account*: Monquhitter.
2 The proverbs quoted here and elsewhere throughout this book are from Cheviot (1896).
3 Herd (1869), vol. 1, p. 129.
4 Heron (1799), vol. 2, p. 226.
5 Child (1882-98), vol. 2, pp. 213-26.
6 *Ibid.*, pp. 454-83.
7 Sillar (1789), p. 132.
8 Ferguson and Roy (1985), p. 28.
9 Kinsley (1968), p. 495.
10 Mayne (1836), p. 24.
11 Banks (1937-41), vol. 1, p. 35.
12 Robertson (1904), p. 128; Kinsley (1968), p. 495.
13 OSA: Kirkpatrick-Juxta.
14 Aiton (1811), pp. 153-54.
15 Campbell (1787), pp. 125-26.
16 Black (1892-93), p. 517.
17 OSA: Kirkmabreck.
18 MacTaggart (1824), p. 210.
19 Melville (1829), p. 290.
20 Cowan and Paterson (2007), p. 505.
21 Ferguson and Roy (1985), vol. 2, p. 269; to John McMurdo, 9 January 1789.
22 Robertson (1904), p. 269; Kinsley (1968), p. 505.
23 *Ibid.* (1904), p. 181; (1968), p. 179.
24 Quoted by Mackay (1992), p. 111.
25 Fenton (2000).
26 Robertson (1904), p. 53; Kinsley (1968), p. 105.
27 Fergusson (1807), p. 249.
28 *Dumfries Weekly Journal*, 8 April 1788, 3b.
29 *Ibid.*, 19 August 1777, 3c.
30 OSA: Kirkmahoe.
31 Davidson (1789), p. 75.
32 OSA: Kirkpatrick-Fleming.
33 Robertson (1904), p. 3; Kinsley (1968), p. 560.

CHAPTER 3

The Deil,
Death and Ghosts

O THOU! whatever title suit thee
Auld Hornie, Satan, Nick, or Clootie,
Wha in yon cavern grim an' sootie,
   Clos'd under hatches,
Spairges about the brunstane cootie, [sprays, dish of brimstone]
   To scaud poor wretches![1] [scald]

THUS Burns addressed the Devil, otherwise Satan, as the chief tormentor in hell, the proponent of sin and the personification of evil: he was the Anti-Christ, and he had to be fought. In the Bible the Devil was as real as any prophet, Christ or the Lord God. The Devil was part of Christian religion, and the Kirk kept belief in him alive.

The Devil lived in Hell, except when he appeared 'going to and fro in the earth, and ... walking up and down in it', as it says in the Book of Job. This precedent made it possible for him to be witnessed in the Scottish countryside. In his appearances, re-told in folk tales, he was often mischievous rather than evil. He was also present through place names such as the Devil's Beef Tub, an ice-formed corrie in the Dumfriesshire hills, the Deil's Putting Stane, a hilltop boulder in Galloway, and the Deil's Dyke, a line of rocks on the beach south of Ayr. And when, in time, he was less feared, his name was applied as a joke: winnowing machines, for example, were said to use the deil's wind.

The Scots had a remarkable number of names for the Devil. In English, he was 'Satan': the word comes from the Arabic, meaning the adversary, and it was a title rather than a personal name. The equivalent was 'the Auld Enemy', which gives an extra dimension to the use of this title by sports journalists for the English. Another Scots name used by Burns was 'Mahoun', from 'Mahomet': this word had been in Scotland by 1475, and probably dates from the time of the Crusades, when all Christian Europe was focused on the Muslims who held the holy city of Jerusalem. From time to time, trade guilds – particularly the hammermen (blacksmiths and other metal workers), and the shoemakers – held processions through the Scottish towns and cities; and as well as figures like the king and the knight in armour, there was often a Turk, standing for the Devil.

Other names, while stopping short of friendliness, give the feeling that the Devil was an accepted member of the community: 'Auld Sym', the 'Auld Ane [one]', the 'Auld Carl' or 'Chiel', 'Auld Harry', or 'Auld Sandy'. All over the English-speaking world he was 'Auld Nick', and 'Auld' implies familiarity. Some names came from his appearance, including 'Auld Hornie' (in Glasgow police officers were 'hornies'), and 'Waghorn'. 'Whaupneb' meant that he had a nose like the long, curved break of the curlew. Each part of the foot of a cloven-hoofed animal is a cloot: thus 'Auld Clootie'. Another common name was 'the Earl o' Hell' which showed that his power was respected, although the expression 'as dark as the Earl o' Hell's waistcoat' also suggests that his power, albeit great, is limited: he was not called the 'Emperor of Hell'.

The name 'Goodman' for the Devil is first found in 1603. It shows a high level of respect, for he had to be propitiated by speaking politely of him. The same idea was behind the laying aside of the corner of a field for him to cultivate: the 'Goodman's croft', 'Goodman's field' (or 'fauld') or 'Clootie's croft'. This patch of land was offered to stop the Devil from blighting the farm,[2] and it was not to be opened with a plough. At harvest, similarly, the corner of a meadow or field of corn was left as an offering to witches – an 'aploch' in Galloway. These pieces of land were the counterpart of 'God's acre' – the churchyard. In north-east Scotland the Devil was also the 'Halyman', and his strip of land the 'Halyman's rig' or 'lye'. Another name was 'Plotcok', from Pluto, the god of the Roman underworld. It also has a suggestion of the Scots word *plot*, to scald, which was used particularly for using boiling water to prepare hides: 'plotcock' implies giving pain.

From time to time the devil appeared to ministers. The following story is about a parish between Lochlea and Kilmarnock, 'among the Craigie hills sae hie' in Burns's words. Mr Campbell of Craigie was active in preaching around his parish, always cautioning his flock against the attentive Satan. Riding home alone he heard his name called but could see no one. Craigie is on top of a bare hill, and we can imagine him looking around the damp stony ground to see who was there. Then laughter broke out, and the voice said, 'The minister himself must harken to the Devil'. Campbell's horse went steadily on and the voice declared that the speaker wished to help the minister, for his wife was at that very moment preparing a poisoned hen for supper. When the roast hen was placed before him on the table the minister wondered how to explain what he had been told. He asked, where had the hen come from? From an old woman 'under a very ill fame for witchcraft'. He gave a piece to a dog, which died.[3]

This appears to show illogical behaviour by the Devil, frustrating the initiative of one of his minions. Perhaps the point is that the Devil is showing off his power to save, or to kill, the righteous. Or perhaps he is demonstrating that he is an unreliable master.[4] He may even be appearing as an angel of light, trying to dupe the faithful.

Ministers encouraged people always to be on the watch for the hand of Satan. Even at the end of the eighteenth century, one minister said his people had often seen the Devil, who 'made wicked attacks' when they were engaged in religious devotion.[5] The action of the Devil also seems to have been a common excuse for the derangement of the loom:

> When the best wark-lume i' the house, [loom]
>   By cantrip wit, [magic]
> Is instant made no worth a louse,
>   Just at the bit.[6]

The loom, along with the mill, and the clock, was the most sophisticated machine in the countryside. It needed constant attention to keep it in order, because to weave was to loosen its many parts. A credulous weaver, like George Ingram at the World's End in Sanquhar, claimed the Devil altered the pattern while he was in the middle of a length of cloth and put his loom out of order.[7] One consequence of being aware of the possibility of diabolical action was that any surprising or unpleasant event might be explained as an act of the Devil. James Makittrick Adair, whose son knew Burns, was a medical student at Edinburgh in the 1750s and took part in a body-snatching expedition to Hamilton in which the corpse was exhumed between the watchman's rounds. The people did not believe it could it have been dug up so quickly, and so said that it was the work of the Devil.[8]

The presence of Satan was a living fear. A century before Burns a Mauchline woman named Marion McColl had been tried for drinking the health of the Devil. She was taken to Edinburgh and scourged at the Netherbow Port. Her erring tongue was bored, her cheek branded, and she was told not to return to Ayrshire on pain of death[9]: her crime may have been that she was conjuring up the Devil, trying to make him appear.

If the Devil is active and present, then there have to be ways of dealing with him. In stories, people were allowed to used any means to trick him. In one widespread tale he made a wager with a farmer that he could cut more corn than him. The night before, the farmer planted hundreds of harrow tines [iron spikes] in the area the Devil was to mow: they blunted the Devil's sickle, and sharpening it slowed him down.[10] In the story of 'The Devil at Little Dunkeld', a village which Burns visited on his Highland tour in 1787, the minister says that he will marry a young woman to a man whom he knows to be the Devil when a candle has been burned to its end: when the end approaches, the minister swallows the candle so that it can never be finished. Thus is the Devil frustrated.[11]

In folklore, the Devil from time to time tried to join a country community, but he could not find a comfortable placing because he was always a poor tradesman. He tried to be a weaver, but gave up after he cut his finger. As an apprentice smith, he pinched his fingers while shoeing a horse. Knowing that he could never have the skill of a mason, he worked for a while as a cowan – a man who builds houses and walls with dry stone, that is without mortar. In the end the Devil found a place as a musician, singing songs in low alehouses, 'much esteemed by that class of men called feckless and debauchees'. The incompetence of the Devil offers us a way of looking at one of the election ballads which Burns wrote in 1796, in which he imaged one of the candidates as a 'trogger', a travelling salesman who sold all sorts of bits and pieces. It ends:

Saw ye e'er sic troggin?
If to buy ye're slack,

> *Hornie's turnin' chapman,*
> *He'll buy a' the pack.*[12]

The trogger's stock is so poor that the inept Satan is willing to take it on.

The word 'devil' was also used to mean an evil spirit, active and troublesome, with a fragment of the Devil's powers, which could take power of an animal or human being. This kind of spirit is in the Bible story of the Gadarene swine, in which Jesus meets 'a certain man, which had devils long time'. The devils say to Jesus that if they are to be cast out from the man, they wish to move to a herd of swine. When they were moved, 'the herd ran violently down a steep place into the sea ... and were choked'.[13] The story was also told of a strict, old-fashioned minister in the Highlands:

> *A clergyman near Balnagown was giving an account of a dreadful*
> *fierce bull which had long troubled his parish, at last he was con-*
> *sulted about taming it, on which he assembled the people, saying*
> *'is there any man here who shaves on sunday, I am sure he does',*
> *pointing to one who look'd conscious. The poor man confess'd*
> *that he had been guilty of that crime once within that twelve-*
> *month; 'Approach' said the parson '& seize the bull'; he obey'd &*
> *the beast was perfectly tractable, on which the parson addressed*
> *his parishioners with 'Behold my brethern the Devil in that man is*
> *stronger than the Devil in the bull'! The bull has behaved well ever*
> *since. The clergyman did not seem to doubt or even to think there*
> *was anything extraordinary in this method of taming.*[14]

Death was quite different from the Devil. The Devil was part of Christian theology, but the figure of Death was a personification of an aspect of life. The ballad 'Death and the Lady', probably written early in the eighteenth century, and certainly known in south-west Scotland, records the conversation between Death and the gentlewoman he has come to collect. She offers him a bribe, and suggests that he could find a prisoner who would welcome the release of death, or someone old whose time has come. She asks to be spared so that she can see her daughter married, and plans to employ doctors:

> *Prepare your cordials, let me comfort find.*
> *My gold shall fly like chaff before the wind.*[15]

Death, however, is inexorable: he knows his professional role. In Burns's poem 'Death and Doctor Hornbook' the skeletal figure of Death is a tradesman. He explains:

Folk maun do something for their bread, [must]
    An' sae maun Death.[16]

Death's natural place is on a headstone in a graveyard, along with his scythe, darts and leister [trident]. This makes him a member of the local community. Like all tradesmen he loves a monopoly and is angered when competition appears, in the form of John Hornbook, to whom we shall return later. And Burns has seen Death on headstones beside Kirk Alloway [see *fig.* 13].

After death, it was possible that the deceased might reappear as a ghost. The existence of ghosts, like the devil and witches, did not have to be explained, for they were in the Bible. A lullaby told children not to be afraid of frightening sounds in the dark:

Wheesht, wheesht, Wullie Moolie, Hushe, Hushe noo my pet,
Hear, hear how he's jinglin the hasp o' the yet.[17] [door]

Moolie meant that the ghost comes from the earth, the mould – and so stems from a dead person who has been buried. Burns described a ghost 'paying thy nocturnal visits to the hoary ruins of decayed Grandeur; or performing thy mystic rites in the shadow of the time-worn Church, while the Moon looks, without a cloud, on the silent, ghastly dwellings of the dead about thee'.[18] This is picturesque but vague: Scottish ghosts usually drew attention to something that was unsatisfactory in the substantial world, such as a crime or an unburied corpse.

The role of the ghost was often to set right some wrong in the past. Gilbert Rule was Principal of Edinburgh University at the end of the seventeenth century and minister of Old Greyfriars: he was astute and learned, with a degree in medicine from Leyden. Travelling north on church business, he arrived at nightfall at the foot of the Cairn o' Mount, one of the paths over the high moors of the eastern Grampians. The inn, half a dozen miles from where William Burnes family had been born near Glenbervie, was full. The landlord offered to supply the Principal with bedding to use in a nearby house which had stood empty for 30 years, for no one would live there. In the night a figure came to Rule's bedside and led him to a stone stair. The following day Rule had the stair dismantled, and a corpse was found. No one at the inn knew anything about it, so Rule called together the local people and addressed them. An old man collapsed and confessed: he had been a mason and had killed a fellow-worker when the house was being built.[19] The ghost enabled a Christian burial for the murdered man.

In Burns's time the story of the Laird of Coul was well known, but it is not easy to know what to make of it.[20] It concerns events in 1721/24, and was the subject of a series of chapbooks which seems to have first been printed about 1740, and often reprinted thereafter. Thomas Maxwell of Coul was a minor laird in the parish of Buittle in Galloway, whose ghost appeared on a road near his house. The story came to the ears of William Ogilvie, a Galloway man who was minister of Innerwick on the East Lothian coast from 1715 to 1729: he said that if Coul had appeared to him, he would have asked about the nature of the afterlife.

Some time later Ogilvie was riding home one evening when a figure on horseback hailed him: the minister said that he thought it was 'collector Castlelaw' and so struck at him with his cane. The reason for this violence is not explained, and the result was surprising, for the cane went through the figure as if it were not there, landing 60 feet away. After this strange start, the apparition identified himself as the Laird of Coul. Ogilvie's first question was 'give me some information about the affairs of the other world, for no man inclines to lose his time in conversing with the dead without having a prospect of hearing and learning something that may be useful'.[21] The apparition was evasive. 'I might profit more by conversing with myself,' said Ogilvie. Coul said that he wanted to arrange the repayment of several sums of money which he had obtained by fraud, and then the apparition rode off with 'a singing and buzzing noise'. Over the next two months he appeared three more times.[22]

At one meeting, the hard-headed Ogilvie asked why Coul had appeared to him, rather than to his own wife? How did Coul imagine Ogilvie was going to convince Mrs Maxwell that he had met the apparition of her husband? Ogilivie said that if he were to relay Coul's requests to his wife, she would be loth to part with money, for there was no written reason why she should. The minister added that if he were to tell brother ministers the story, they would respond that he had met the Devil, and would imply that anything said by Coul's shade would almost certainly be a lie. He ended by telling Coul not to send him on 'an April errand' – not to make him an April fool.

We should be wary of believing this story: Ogilvie may have made it up. One of Coul's claims was that his horse was Andrew Johnstoun, who had been his tenant: this sounds like a variation on the idea that witches' steeds were human, and lends weight to the idea that Ogilvie was re-using a piece of well-known popular belief. According to the chapbook version of the story, Ogilvie was said to have died soon after meeting the ghost, though in reality it was five years and this also sounds like the use of an old formula to give credibility to the supernatural aspect. Whatever had happened in Galloway, one is inclined to regard Ogilvie's statement as a thought experiment, an answer to the question, 'What would I say if I met a ghost?' Ogilvie is giving a clever and indirect argument against the existence of ghosts. And he is suggesting that if they do exist, they are powerless and pointless.

The Laird of Coul was the most visible ghost in eighteenth-century Scotland. Because of the popularity of chapbooks, he was known all over the Lowlands. Yet the dramatic story was only part of the chapbook – the rest was a theological discussion of the nature of the afterlife. After Coul's time, the ghost was less frightening.

The final group of supernatural appearances relates to the approach of death. Lives were short, accidents common, and with little understanding of disease many people were rather unwell, or in some form of decline, before the period of acute illness which preceded death. People were said to be 'fey' when they were fated to die soon. In the song 'The Battle of Sherramuir', Burns says that 'fey men died' – they were the men who were bound by fate to lose their lives.[23] People were usually fey because they had in some way been in contact with the supernatural: it was as though a door had been opened and they were about to pass through it.

The appearance of various lights were indications that death was approaching: a nurse who saw a light about her head and shoulders knew it was a sign that she would die soon.[24] The *deid-cannle* was a light glimpsed for a moment, indoors or outdoors, sometimes moving from the house of the person who was to die, to the kirkyard. The *deid-fire*, also known as the 'red kelpies' was St Elmo's fire, and it presaged death at sea. After death, the *deid-licht* was a light visible above the corpse. Sometimes two dogs, black and white, were seen, fighting for possession of the soul.[25] A wraith was the apparition of a living person: its appearance meant that death was imminent.

The Devil had nothing to do with the choice of those who were to die, or the process of dying. At the burials of those who had sold him their souls, he intervened to make his claim. There was a story of a funeral party on the moorland road from Moniaive to Dalry who were joined by a stranger who accompanied them to the kirkyard, and there the soul was his. The burn at which he met the party was labelled 'Bargain Stream', from the bargain which the dead man had made with Satan.[26]

And so we can take our leave of Burns and the Devil:

> *But fare you weel, auld Nickie-ben!*
> *O wad ye tak a thought an' men'!*
> *Ye aiblins might – I dinna ken –*
> *   Still hae a stake:*
> *I'm wae to think upo' yon den,*
> *   Ev'n for your sake!*[27]

In other words, Burns sympathises with the Devil, stuck in his smoky Hell, and wonders whether he might 'Still hae a stake', still have a chance of reforming, or of seeing a better side to himself.

NOTES

1   Robertson (1904), p. 71; Kinsley (1968), p. 168.
2   MacPherson (1929), p. 141.
3   Wodrow (1842-43), vol. 4, p. 110.
4   *Ibid.*
5   *Old Statistical Account*: Tongland.
6   Robertson (1904), p. 73; Kinsley (1968), p. 170.
7   Wilson (1904), pp. 97-102.
8   Adair (1790), p. 18.
9   Edgar (1885-86), p. 261.
10 Briggs (1970), vol. 3, pp. 76-77.
11 *Ibid.*
12 Robertson (1904), p. 418; Kinsley (1968), p. 78.
13 Mark 5:13.
14 Letter from Frances Mackenzie to her sister, 6 November 1809, National Archives of Scotland, GD 46/15/19.
15 From a broadside, National Library of Scotland, L.C. fol. 70 (52).
16 Robertson (1904), p. 64; Kinsley (1968), p. 81.
17 Abercromby (1894).
18 Ferguson and Roy (1985), vol. 2, p. 145.
19 Wodrow (1842-43), vol. 4, pp. 88-90.
20 This account of the Laird of Coul is taken from Wood (1911), pp. 344-55 and 18th-century chapbooks.
21 *Ibid.*, p. 348.
22 On the road from Oldhamstocks, and on the post road from Old Camus, at the head of Pease path.
23 Robertson (1904), p. 401; Kinsley (1968), p. 535.
24 Wodrow (1842-43), vol. 2, p. 143.
25 Heron (1799), vol. 1, p. 227.
26 Gregor (1898), p. 490.
27 Robertson (1904), p. 75; Kinsley (1968), p. 172.

CHAPTER 4

Witches, Spirits
and other Curious Things

She prophesied that, late or soon,
Thou would be found, deep drown'd in Doon;
Or catch'd wi' warlocks in the mirk,
By Alloway's auld, haunted kirk.[1]

A VARIETY OF witches and spirits were in action in the Scottish countryside. Part of their purpose was to express fears: of the dangers of riding on a moonless night, of the failure of a year's crop, or the sudden death of a member of the family. As a result, it was possible to take action to protect oneself, or one's cattle, say, against these malign forces. These fears were not clearly defined, so witches and the supernatural beings who represented them did not have clear or consistent characteristics.

A human being became a witch by selling her (or his) soul to the Devil in return for various kinds of power and sometimes wealth. The nature of the power decreased over the centuries. In earlier days there had been some senior witches, gyre-carlins, who only appeared between Candlemas and Fastern's E'en. Their powers were enormous: one even dried out an inlet of the sea to make Lochar Moss, east of Dumfries, an area of perhaps ten square miles. By Burns's time their abilities were more limited, and sometimes their occult knowledge was called upon to solve problems. For example, it was alleged before Mauchline kirk session that a man had sought a 'spell woman' to 'cast the cards in order to find who had stolen the lawn'.[2] She was said to have used playing cards to detect who had stolen some fine linen.

The characterisation of someone as a witch made unwelcome happenings seem to have a real cause, one which could be talked about. But once a witch had been named, there was an unhappy temptation to confront her or him: this was partly to save the witch's soul, but also to punish. It says in Exodus, 'Thou shalt not suffer a witch to live', and there were executions for witchcraft in Scotland until 1727. This was the last act in a vicious witch craze, a compound of persecution, guilt, accusations, confessions, burning and hanging. As Robert Cromek, the song collector, later noted: 'So eager were they to destroy Satan's dominion on earth, that the bloodhounds of religious law were uncoupled, and the witches hunted down by their smell.'[3]

However, the fascination with witches lingered. One of the first books printed at Paisley (1775) was about Christian Shaw of Bargarran, a laird's daughter who accused various people of harming her by spells. This eleven-year-old had been responsible for the deaths of seven people.

The witch related to the instability of life – the threats which lay under the thin ice of social interaction. For example, the ballad 'Allison Gross' is about a witch who wants to marry a man who refuses to co-operate. She turns him into an 'ugly worm', or in more general terms, humiliates him and stops him from living his own life. The man is finally set free by the Queen of the Fairies on Halloween, the one day on which she had the power to do this.

By the middle of the eighteenth century witches' more extreme powers had disappeared, yet those identified as such could still, without working, enjoy a supply of malt, meal, cheese and milk, given by people who feared the witch. Young men gladly cut peat for them in the hope of favourable intervention in love affairs. A Mauchline merchant complained that a woman had cursed him so he would not thrive and his cattle would die. Under questioning she admitted that she had said she hoped his cow would die, but no more than that. Complaint dismissed. However, she made the counter-charge that the merchant's wife had falsely accused her, including the opinion that the wife should be 'bled above the eyes', meaning that a cross should be cut in her forehead with a knife or nail, in other words that the accuser was a witch. The merchant had a daughter, Jean Markland, one of Burns's 'Mauchline belles'.[4]

With only vague ideas about the power of the witch, any task that proved more difficult than expected could be said to have been bewitched, like milk being slow to 'turn' to butter despite muscle-aching work at the plunger-churn:

> *Thence country wives, wi' toil an' pain,*
> *May plunge an' plunge the kirn in vain;*
> *For oh! the yellow treasure's taen*
>   *By witchin' skill.*[5]

Witches were usually based firmly in their locality and their activities related to its specific topography. The witch from Caerlaverock met her colleague from New Abbey in the middle of the River Nith to plan their mischievous activities. The latter used a magic boat which normally had the appearance of a horse's skull, kept buried in sand beside the river, which she changed into an elaborately decorated vessel. Willie Wilken, a famous witch in Nithsdale, continued to curl after his death, 'to the great terror and annoyance of the neighbourhood, not much regarding whether the loch be frozen or not'.[6] The shouts of the curlers, and the roaring of the stones on the ice, were heard.

A story from Annandale shows the context in which witchery operated. A man named Little became engaged to marry a woman whose family he did not know, but the day before the wedding he discovered that her mother was a witch, so he called off the ceremony. The witch took offence at her daughter being rejected, and tormented Little. He was so oppressed that he emigrated to America, and the determined witch went too. Even so, the supernatural diaspora did not last: the miserable man returned home, and the witch came with him. When he was at Mein Mill, downstream from Ecclefechan, the witch in the form of a giant cat made him fall into the grinding mechanism where he was crushed. His burial took place in the old graveyard at Pennersaughs.[7] This we can interpret as follows: the man tried to escape to America, which may be taken to mean the modern world, but failed; he was killed by traditional technology; and he is held in the past by interment in a place which has been used for the purpose for centuries.

The fictional story of Sawney Bean, the Scottish cannibal, was written in London early in the eighteenth century, and printed in the *Newgate Calendar*, a collection of sensational stories about crime and executions.[8] Bean was said to have lived in a cave on the Ayrshire coast, killing and eating passing travellers, whose disappearance was blamed on several innkeepers who were executed. Finally, an intended victim escaped and the king appeared with an armed force. Bean, his wife, 14 children and 32 grandchildren, all unrepentant, were put to death with appropriate cruelty. The story spoke to the reader's fear of lonely places and the unknown people who live there: it is about the thin skin of civilisation and the raw savagery which might lie beneath. In most versions of the story, Sawney came from Galloway, but in one the name is printed as Galway (perhaps a slip), and in another he is called John Gregg and placed in Devon – three remote locations. Unspeakable crime, written out in detail, always attracts attention, and to the eighteenth-century mind the idea of dying unrepentant, of refusing to confess and make one's peace with one's Maker, was a shocking blasphemy. It was surely devilry or witchcraft.

A range of strategies were used to protect people and animals from the ill-will of witches. The most common was to place a cross of rowan twigs tied with red thread over the door on Beltane or Rood Day. In Galloway, crosses were replaced by sprigs or bunches of berries, the cross being unwelcome since it was taken to be a symbol used by the Catholic Church. Rowan trees were often planted beside houses. A double hazelnut – two nuts growing in one husk – was another form of protection, called a St John's nut. In the nineteenth and early twentieth centuries it was common to decorate the threshold with a pattern of knots in pipe clay, and this was said to make a barrier which witches could not cross.[9] A minister gave an English traveller to the Highlands a stone like a cat's eye from Iona, a charm against all evil.[10] This sounds like an agate (although it may have been a piece of polished marble). Burns had, as we have seen [fig. 28], a set of agate waistcoat buttons.

The way to remove a witch's power was to 'score abune the breath', as mentioned above, and it was still being done at the beginning of the nineteenth century. At Wigtown Sheriff Court there was a trial for assault in 1825, after a 'witch' had received head wounds. The following year a man at Annan, believing that his wife had been bewitched and that an old woman walking past their home had been responsible, threw the unfortunate woman to the ground and cut across her forehead with a knife.[11] About the same time, a farmer's wife in Corrie in Eastern Dumfriesshire, sick and delirious, claimed she had been bewitched by Jenny, a local carlin, and two female relatives of the sufferer went to Jenny and scored her brow with a large knife, a 'lang kale gully'.[12]

There were various spirits in the Scottish countryside. The *gyre* was a monster, a powerfully malignant spirit, usually a woman.[13] The *worri-cow* was a hobgoblin or demon, or sometimes the Devil himself, as when Robert Fergusson wrote about 'warlocks loupin' [jumping or dancing] round the worrikow'.[14] The first part of the word means to worry in the sense of to harass, and a *cow* is a hobgoblin. The *famh*, from the Gaelic word for a mole, was a beast larger than a mole, which emerged on summer mornings to leave a kind of glutinous matter which killed horses. The *erd hund* [earth hound] was a mysterious animal which dug in graveyards: by implication, it ate corpses.

Bogle is a Scots word for something like a ghost. Fergusson described Greyfriars kirkyard in Edinburgh thus:

> ... *at mirkest hour,*
> *Bogles and spectres wont to take their tour.*[15]

He is saying that the bogle was similar to a ghost, but distinct from it. *Bogle* also meant an entity which was similar to a ghost, but had more powers, such as the ability to cause harm, a kind of minor devil. Burns addressed the supernatural source of his own inspiration, wondering what kind of creature it was, but recognising its power: 'Be thou a Bogle by the eerie side of an auld thorn, in the dreary glen through which herd-callan maun bicker in his gloaming route frae the fauld!'[16]

The *kelpie* usually took the form of a grey horse, luring people into the water to drown. Kelpies were often active at fords, and many disappeared when bridges became common. Burns wrote of them 'haunting the ford, or ferry, in the starless night, mixing thy laughing yell with the howling of the storm, & roaring of the flood, as thou viewest the perils & miseries of Man on the foundering horse, or in the tumbling boat!'[17] Equally dramatic was the way in which the Devil acted through his agents, to drown people who tried to cross frozen water:

> *When thowes dissolve the snawy hoord,* [thaws, hoard]
> *An' float the jinglin' icy-boord,*
> *Then water-kelpies haunt the foord,*
> *By your direction,*
> *An' 'nighted trav'llers are allur'd*
> *To their destruction.*[18]

The other widespread water spirit was the *shelly coat*, half fish and half cow, that lived in inland lochs. James Graham of Claverhouse, the hunter of Covenanters, was said to have protected himself with a coat of shelly coat skins, held together by the bones of water snakes. This was said to be the reason why he could not be harmed by a lead bullet; a silver one had to be used to kill him.

The devious Devil also deployed lights to decoy the confused traveller in the dark, a traveller like Tam o' Shanter. A *spunkie* was a will o' the wisp, 'seen mostly in bogish myrish ground, in louring, foulsom, unwholsom weather'.[19]

> *An' aft your moss-traversing spunkies*
> *Decoy the wight that late an' drunk is:*
> *The bleezin, curst, mischievous monkies*
>   *Delude his eyes,*
> *Till in some miry slough he sunk is,*
>   *Ne'er mair to rise.*[20]

Burns's granny told him that the Devil rode on a spunkie.

Fairies were unlike the Devil and witches: they do not appear in the Bible. Fairies had other names which give some idea of how they were seen: 'peaceable people', 'guid neibours', or *seelie wichts* (lucky or happy wights). They were, however, linked to the Devil by being required to give a 'teind tae hell' every seven years, the payment of one of their own, or if possible a human whom they had captured as a substitute. Fairies lived under roots of thorn bushes: blackthorn was the 'fairy tree' in Galloway, and their activities were related to the calendar: they rode on Beltane and at Halloween. It was unlucky to carry its blossom into a house, and people left gifts for them on Halloween. At Kilcormack, above the Galloway Dee, the fairies ground meal with help from departed spirits, where the kirkyard and mill were close together. Elves were originally a rather different kind of being, but by the eighteenth century 'elf' was another name for fairy.

Although fairies were not ill disposed towards the human race (or perhaps they were simply not particularly interested in them), they could perform vicious tricks when irritated. On the Loch of Edingham, near Dalbeattie, curlers finished their game at dusk, but as they were leaving the fairies appeared. The curlers who stayed to watch went onto the ice, and when the last of them was well away from bank the ice cracked and 21 people drowned.

On the other hand, fairies could show gratitude. A story was widespread of a fairy asking a housewife for food, receiving it, and responding by magically ensuring that her meal girnal was never empty. There is a similar tale of a man walking past the conical hill of Ruberslaw, east of Hawick, who saw nothing, but heard a voice say, 'There's a bairn born, but nae sark [shirt] tae pit on't'. He took off his shirt and it was snatched away, and he prospered for the rest of his life. Unlike those in the east, fairies in the West of Scotland were mild, generous and forgiving.[21]

Fairies were so fond of human children that from time to time they stole them, and substituted another being for the child – a changeling. Changelings looked identical to the children they replaced, but their behaviour was subtly different and less satisfactory. They were disliked. The English writer on witchcraft, Reginald Scot, complained of the terror of the supernatural: 'They have so fraied us [made us afraid] with elves, hags ... changelings ... and other such bugs, that we are afraid of our own shadowes'.[22] Unbaptised infants were particularly attractive to fairies: these children were 'uncanny' (the word passed from Scots to English), meaning that they were in contact with the spirit world until they were separated from it by the ritual of baptism.[23]

In the ballad 'Tam Lin' the hero was once human, but when out hunting he falls and is captured by the Queen of the Fairies and thus becomes one of the fairy court. When he makes Janet, a mortal, pregnant, she is determined to regain him from the fairy world. Her one chance to do this is on Halloween, when the fairies come out of their hidden home and ride through the world. Tam explains to Janet that she must pull him from his horse as he passes. The first time she tries he will turn into a savage, the next time a snake, and the third time a red-hot iron. Like many ballads, 'Tam Lin' is a mixture of the mystic and the practical: it is based on the sexual longing of Janet and Tam, on her needing a father for her child, and her knowledge that Tam is a laird's son. In the last verse the Elfin Queen, too, reveals her emotions:

> But had I kend, Tam Lin, she says,
> What now this night I see,
> I would hae taen out thy twa grey een,
> And pit in twa een o' tree.[24] [wood]

Fairies also lived in places that were difficult to reach, such as Crichhope Linn, in Nithsdale, near Closeburn. It was:

inaccessible in a great measure to real beings, this linn was consid-ered as the habitation of imaginary ones; and at the entrance to it, there was a curious cell or cave, called the Elf's Kirk, where accor-ding to the superstition of the times, the imaginary inhabitants of the linn were supposed to hold their meetings. The darkness of the place, upon which the sun never shines; the ragged rocks, rising above one's head ... with here and there a blasted tree, bursting from the crevices; the rumbling of the water falling from rock to rock, and forming deep pools; together with some degree of danger to the spectator.[25]

More common were the distinctive rounded hills that opened up to give access to the fairies' meeting places – like Burnswark near Lock-erbie, Ruberslaw, and Cassilis Downans near Mount Oliphant, which Burns mentions in 'Halloween'.

The idea of the 'elf-arrow' dealt with two strange things: the unpre-dictability of animal health, and the occasional finding in the fields of small, beautifully-worked arrowheads [see *fig. 30*]. In the eighteenth century they were thought to be bolts fired by fairies at cattle. In fact they had been made by human beings in the Stone Age, many centuries before the birth of Christ.[26] There was a method for testing whether an animal was cured of being elf-shot. A burning peat was placed on the threshold of the byre, and the cow driven out. If she walked quietly she was still ill; but if she 'lets a spang over it with a billy – jumps over it and lows – then she is cured'.[27] The elf-shot could be cured by passing a horseshoe three times round the cow, and feeding the animal *elf-girse* [grass] or Lady's mantle.[28] Alternatively, the beast could be touched with an elf-arrow, or given water to drink, in which the arrow had been dipped.

The belief in elf-arrows continued after Burns's time, particularly in areas where farming was moving more slowly into the rational world in which explanations had to be based on material things which could be seen. In Caithness in the nineteenth century, the elf-shot cow was one which breathed hard and had no appetite. Someone with the skill, typically an old woman, searched the hide to find holes in the layer underneath it, bathing them with salt water, and then a little salt water was poured into the animal's ears and rather more down her throat.[29] In Sutherland in the 1860s, a man was shown a dead cow that had been elf-shot. He suggested that the animal had rolled over and her long horns had gone deep into the soil and pinned her there: the response was that this was common when a beast had been struck by an elf-bolt.[30]

One spirit was good natured – the brownie. It has been said that the brownie was the opposite of the fairy, being dark rather than fair, solitary rather than sociable, hard-working, and living most of the time in the mortal world. The brownie was a shaggy household sprite, who if treated well did the housework while the servants were asleep. As Burns put it, addressing one of his friends as though he was a brownie, he was 'set, at dead of night, to thy task by the blazing ingle, or in the solitary barn ... as thou performest the work of twenty of the sons of men ere the cock-crowing summon thee to thy ample cog [bowl] of substantial brose!'[31]

The psychology of belief in brownies relates to the medieval idea of the Land of Cockaigne, a kind of early paradise where food was plentifully available without having to work for it. The brownie was considered loyal: one in a Royalist household in Galloway attacked a Cromwellian soldier.[32] But they disliked lavish rewards such as fine food or a suit of smart clothes. If an attempt was made to give anything like this, the brownie left and did not return. The underlying message was that people should behave in a way that is appropriate to their station and role in life, and that people should treat others in a like manner. The implication is conservative: the world should never change.

Supernatural activity was not spread evenly over the country, and in some places it was particularly dense. Above Sanquhar, the Crawick Water falls into the Nith from the east, draining the big, bleak, rounded Lowther Hills. The people there were supposed to be so religious that no one devil could 'keep his credit', so a colony of them were based there, fought by the human inhabitants with prayers, psalms and texts. One night a man became separated from his friends when crossing the Crawick Water: they heard hideous yelling and then his severed limbs were seen floating over the trees. Traces of blood were to be seen for years on the rocks in the burn.[33] One stretch of the Crawick had the Witch's Crag, the Deil's Chair and the Deil's Stane, and a tributary called the Haunted Linn where a man in black walked, the Devil himself. A remorseful white lady was to be seen nearby: she had been betrothed to a Covenanter, transferred her affections to a military man and told him when a conventicle was to be held. When the troops moved on it, her first lover was killed, and by accident or purpose she drowned.[34]

In the matter-of-fact world it was more difficult to believe stories in which witches changed their shape. There was an old tale about Allanhaugh, a hamlet in the Border hills, where it was known that, when a strong wind blew suddenly on Saturday night, the Devil was visiting a local witch. Two men decided to investigate. They climbed the gable of her house and looked down the chimney, watching a dozen large grey cats arrive, each walking three times round the Devil and then:

> *Takin' their tails in their teeth, tumblit heels owre heid and startled up auld liart carlins* [grey-haired women], *wi mous moupin'* [mouths twitching] *like maukins in May.*[35]

One observer said in 1820 that there were no longer real witches who took their power from the Devil, although ill-wishers and uncanny folk did still exist.[36] Some of those with a name for witchcraft saw this as a desirable reputation. Euphemia Stevenson, for example, known as Eppie Sooty, was called a 'vulpinary [fox-like] veteran of the black art'. However, despite her threats to stop cows' milk and to prevent hens from laying, she was in fact a fake who tried to maintain the appearance of a witch by wearing a black cloak with a large hood.[37]

It was no longer necessary to crush an eggshell to stop a witch from using it as a boat, or to bind red thread round farming tools so that a witch could not frustrate the work done with them, or to carry an ear of wheat in the pocket because each grain bore the face of Christ who gave protection against the Devil. Shrewd people, however, recognised that the supernatural could cause harm in the real world simply because people believed in it. James Makittrick Adair, the father of a friend of Burns, told the story of William Burt, governor of the Leeward Islands. Burt hosted a dinner, at which a phantom was seen by one of the company; the guest said that one of those present would soon die. The governor was taken ill, brooded and expired. Adair's realistic comment was: 'Superstition cannot be excluded, even from the strongest minds, and many have been lost by its influence.'

John MacTaggart, the gossipy author of the *Scottish Gallovidian Encyclopedia* (1824), wrote that 'the Scots are a nation not only famous for religion, war, learning and independence, but also superstition'. It is not clear what he meant, but since his time some Scots words relating to the supernatural have become more generally used, even if this has not given Scotland a fame for superstition. In the Middle Ages the English word 'grammar' meant, as it does today, the study of the rules of language, but it also stood for a sophisticated level of learning. In Scotland it was varied to 'glamour', meaning a magic spell, and sometimes a beauty which was so great that it cast a spell over people who experienced it. Hollywood turned it into the physical attraction of stars on the silver screen. *Eldrich* was an old word meaning ghastly, hideous or unnatural. Burns used the word in the 'Elegy on Captain Matthew Henderson', addressing

> *Ye houlets, frae your ivy bow'r,*
> *In some auld tree, or eldritch tow'r*[38]

And Death, in 'Death and Dr Hornbook' 'grain'd [groaned] an eldritch laugh'.[39] To 'have the reid hand' meant that a criminal had the evidence, physical or supernatural, of his crime about him. Walter Scott turned the phrase into 'red-handed', and through him it passed into the English language.

Burns said that his nurse, Betty Davidson, had told him

> *... tales and songs concerning devils, ghosts, fairies, brownies,*
> *witches, warlocks, apparitions, cantraips, giants, inchanted*
> *towers, dragons and other trumpery.*[40]

Most of these had been in Scots for a long time, but dragons and enchanted towers were trumpery introduced from England. English ideas also affected the ways in which some people saw witches. For example, the idea that they rode on broomsticks, 'virl'd [with a ferrule, i.e. a ring round the end of the stick] with a dead man's bones', using stirrup irons which were the collar bones of the she wolf, with saddle bags made from the scalps of unchristened children.[41] Scots witches rode horses, so this was an alien notion, if not an invention.

MacTaggart tells us of the aged Andrew Sproat who lived at Millhall, on the west side of Kirkcudbright Bay. Andrew said:

> *Hech how, there's nae fun ava now amang the fowk; they're a'*
> *grown as serious as our auld minister wont to be at a sacrament;*
> *nae meetings at ithers ingles to sing sangs, and tell divertin tales,*
> *nae boggles [bogles] now to be seen about Hell's-Hole and the*
> *Ghaistcraft; nae witchwives about the clench [cleuch, i.e. narrow*
> *gorge], nor warlocks about the Shellin Hill o' Kirkaners.*[42]

We can take two points from this. First, the changes that made Scotland a world leader in agricultural methods, and made lairds wealthy and farmers better off, were to the disadvantage of many working people. The new methods enabled the worker to be deployed effectively the whole year round; there were no quiet periods as there had been in midsummer, and after the harvest. In the fermtoun all the men had been more or less equal, but now there were masters and servants. The second point is that superstition had declined, and it had given not only colour to socialising, but also to late night journeys home from social occasions. The countryside had been alive; there had been an unseen multitude of bogles and witches, but rural depopulation affected supernatural as well as human beings.

The lifetimes of William Burnes and his son Robert cover the years when the general belief in the supernatural steadily disappeared. Elizabeth Mure of Caldwell, a member of an Ayrshire landed family, said that when she was a girl in the 1720s 'few old houses was without a Ghost chamber that few people has the Courage to sleep in. Omens and Dreams were much regarded even by people of the best Education.'[43] Part of the basis for these beliefs was 'the power of the Devil and Hell', but in time religion was separated from the power of the Devil and the fear of hell: 'those terrors began to wear off and religion appear'd in a more ammiable light. We were bid draw our knowledge of God from his works, the Chief of which was the Soul of a good man.'[44] By 1750 landed families felt that their children should not be brought up with stories which they believed were old-fashioned: 'nurses was turned off who would tell the young of Witches and Ghosts.' When Dr Johnson visited Scotland, he noted, 'It is in the common talk of the Lowland *Scots*, that the Notion of the *Second Sight* is wearing away with other superstitions; and that its reality is no longer supposed, but by the grossest people'.[45] Country folk were left to face the future without the familiar bogle or the kindly brownie.

The English antiquary John Aubrey believed that technology had killed the supernatural: 'The divine art of Printing and Gunpowder have frighted away Robin Goodfellow and the fairies.'[46] Machines and structures gave the feeling that human power could dominate nature, like the new bridges at Ayr and Dumfries, and make things which nature could not, like the output of the new textile mills. People were also becoming wealthier.

The spirit of credulity, which rises out of ignorance ... is now greatly worn away; and the belief in witches, in fairies, and other ideal beings, is generally dying out. ... Servility of mind, the natural consequence of poverty and oppression, has lost much of its hold. ... Not only the farmers, but many of the tradesmen, read the news-papers, and take an interest in the measures of government.[47]

The supernatural had been displaced from the people's mind by something which was supposed to be more rational – parliament.

In the past, the weather had been a constant source of interest. Even if crops thrived, would they be ruined at harvest? This was a central concern to the whole community: if there was not enough food, people would starve. More effective farming and better breeds of corn made famine less likely. However, when it did threaten, the embryonic local government was effective enough to import food, and this happened in parts of Scotland in the 1780s. Farm workers were still paid partly in meal, but the cash economy was growing, and this brought a new source of fear: what if I do not have the money to buy the food I need, and to rent a home? The Devil and witches had no answer to this question, and responses like working hard and saving money had nothing to do with the supernatural.

The continuing belief in the supernatural depended on the conviction that there was something out there in the dark. A proverb said, 'The day hes eyne [eyes], the night hes ears' – a sound was the stimulus for the idea that there were supernatural beings active in the landscape. Thus in Burns's poem 'Halloween' the widow Leezie goes to the spot – by implication, a lonely one – where 'three lairds' lands met at a burn', to soak her sleeve in the water, expecting to see in the wet fabric the face of her next husband. But instead she thinks that she has encountered the Devil.

> *Amang the brachens on the brae,* [bracken]
>   *Between her an' the moon,*
> *The Deil, or else an outler quey,* [cow which spends the winter outside]
>   *Gat up an' gae a croon:*
> *Poor Leezie's heart maist lap the hool;* [leaped over the little hill]
>   *Near lav'rock height she jumpit,* [the height of the lark's flight]
> *But miss'd a fit, an' in the pool,*
>   *Out-owre the lugs she plumpit,* [over the ears she plunged]
>   *Wi' a plunge that night.*[48]

'Lap the hool' has the implication of jumping right over a fairy knoll.

The Devil was also active in the fields, usually unseen but making alarming and inexplicable noises – inexplicable unless they were made by a malignant force.

> When twilight did my grannie summon,
> To say her pray'rs, douce, honest woman! [sedate]
> Aft yont the dyke she's heard you bummin',
>   Wi' eerie drone;
> Or, rustlin', thro' the boortrees comin', [elder bushes]
>   Wi' heavy groan.[49]

These sounds called up half-shaped fears which ranged from assault to misty premonitions that something was going to go wrong.

'The day has eyene, the night has ears' – and one might add that the mind has fears. A Galloway man said that the sound that an owl made when resting in summer shadows was a moaning 'huam'. When a boy he had wondered what it was:

> I had some work before I found the sound proceeded from the owl; the people about me said, as no doubt their ancestors had done, that the sound 'was the humming o' boggles i' the dark green wud'.[50]

Owls, night birds, feathered predators, had a sinister ability to see in the near-dark.

Superstition was also killed by the belief that people could take control of the world, and bend nature to their will. In a landscape that was free from fences and walls, animals like cats and hares moved easily, silent and watchful, and it was simple to imagine nameless animals, half-formed in the mist, shapeless, subtle and sudden. People and spirits could move over the open countryside, but the rectangular field and its gates limited the places to hide. Other changes were more brutal. There was a cave in Nithsdale associated with the fairies:

> This cave proving a good freestone-quarry, has lately been demolished, for the purpose of building houses, and from the abode of elves, has been converted into habitations for men.[51]

In the Highlands, near Aberfeldy, there was a huge boulder by the road. Dew collected on top of it, and the pool of water was regarded as a healing well. In road improvement the boulder was not merely removed: it was blown up. The countryside was redesigned by the building of new roads and bridges. Drainage ditches and waterwheels, like the famous one Lord Kames had built on Flanders Moss on the River Forth, changed the substance of the soil. New mansion houses were built with open views, and as a result they could be seen – and their power felt – from a distance. The new farming methods produced enough food to enable the cities to grow, and farmers ceased to be victims of the natural world, but people might work in harmony with it, the better to control it. In the slow and predictable countryside, one might wonder what was going on beneath the surface, but in the industrial world people had to deal with the surface. The hidden world of the supernatural had been leached away.

The Chevalier Taylor, a famous quack doctor, talking about the importance of his trade as an eye surgeon, called the eye 'that most amazing, that stupendous, that comprehending, that incomprehensible, that miraculous organ – The eye has dominion over all things. The eye was made for the world and the world for the eye'.[52] In the second half of the eighteenth century the British, and the Scots particularly, became eye-aware as never before, and increasingly related to their surroundings through visual experiences, then recording what they saw in words and images. Landscape paintings and engravings became popular.

Precise observation was valued. Maria Riddell, a friend of Burns who was married to the brother of Robert Riddell, his neighbour when he lived at Ellisland, wrote a book about her voyages to Madeira and the West Indies. She looked closely and wrote clearly.

> *The Portuguese are extremely dark complexioned, but have fine eyes and teeth; the women are in general handsome; the lower class of people are indolent, dirty, and much addicted to theft; they are very musical, and extremely gallant. You seldom pass a night at Madeira without hearing a serenade of guitars and mandolines in some part of the street.*[53]

Burns himself was a brilliant observer and descriptive writer, when he chose to be. On his Border tour he rode to Dunbar with Nancy Sherriff, who had

an old, dun carthorse that once had been fat; a broken old side
saddle, without crupper, stirrup, or girth; a bridle that in former
times had had buckles, and a crooked meandring hazle stick which
might have borne a place with credit in a scrubbed besom.[54]

He did not use this talent often, preferring to deploy his psychological
insight.

People started to take much more interest in the visual appearance
of buildings. The Ayr tolbooth, with which Burns would have been
familiar, was lumpy and obstructive: the replacement of 1832, with its
delicate spire, feels like a reaction. Farm buildings which had huddled in
the landscape were now rebuilt on top of hills; and larger windows
changed the relationship between the farm and its outlook. Big houses
such as the palatial Culzean Castle (1777) were built to look as though
they owned the landscape. Communal buildings, too, were a matter of
pride. The engraved metal badges that gave subscribers admission to the
Theatre Royal at Dumfries had on them an elevation of the theatre.

Ministers complained that young servant women were spending
their wages, sometimes the entire amount, on cloth and clothes. All were
more aware of their appearance. When the Dumfries draper William
Corrie died in 1777, his executors advertised plain, striped and flowered
lutestrings [silks] and muslins, cambrics, lawns, linens, shalloons [lighter
woollens], cashmeres, crepes, satins and durants – a wide range of
textiles that had been available for a century and more, but now they
were cheaper. Burns had mocked 'men three-parts made by tailors and
barbers'. His uniform for the Royal Dumfries Volunteers was a blue coat
with white facings, a white waistcoat, knee-breeches, stockings, and a
round hat with a black feather. It cost £7-4/-. Burns received the account
while he was at Brow, out of funds and dying.

Maps were a visualisation on paper of the countryside. The first
detailed map of Ayrshire to be published was by the Armstrongs, father
and son, in 1775, simplifying its corrugations, emphasising the rivers:
'every valley shall be exalted, and every mountain and hill shall be laid
low.' The map assembled data, but its clarity was the result of leaving
out almost all the human aspects, like the cairn 'where hunters fand the
murdered bairn', and it made no distinction between land that was under
cultivation, and rough pasture. Its plain delineation, however, left no
room for the idea that some land had special qualities, like the 'faintie
grund' or 'hungry grun', which caused an individual suddenly to feel

hungry; or for the idea that butter made from the milk of cows which had been grazed in a churchyard was a cure for consumption.

Twenty years before the Armstrongs' map, a huge survey of Scotland had been completed under the direction of William Roy. During the Jacobite rebellion the army had realised that they had little knowledge of the topography of Scotland. As a young soldier Roy had been involved in road-making in the Scottish Highlands after the 1745 Rebellion. He called his map 'a magnificent military sketch', and it is preserved as a manuscript in London in the British Library. By the 1770s Roy's conception of mapping had moved from sketching to the use of instruments with new degrees of rigour. He said:

> ... it is not until things have been viewed in every possible light, that the errors, even of our own experiments, are discovered, the points in question ultimately ascertained, and the branches of philosophy depending upon them, gradually brought nearer to perfection.[55]

Perhaps the relentless pursuit is not of hidden truth, but of hidden error, and stems from his Calvinism.

Headstones were rare in kirkyards before the late seventeenth century. After that, most carried lettering but little else. However, a minority bore carving, particularly symbols, and they are important and often overlooked parts of the people's history. Not only did each one commemorate a local man or family, they were also enjoyed and understood by the whole community.

Some symbols on headstones were about the transition from life to death, and to the eternal life beyond. The angel was the most common symbol, sometimes a full length figure but more often a head with wings. It carried the soul to heaven. Other symbols emphasised the value of life, like Adam and Eve; they represented not only the continuation of the human race generation after generation, they were also a reminder of the existence of sin, a particular enthusiasm of the period.

Regeneration and growth were also represented by the Green Man, of which there is a fine and rare example at Alloway, rising from the Earth [see *fig.* 14]. He stood for the cyclical pattern in the year, the new foliage in spring, the dying back in autumn, and winter as 'the deid o' the year'. At the same time the colour green was linked with death: the green lady, for example, was a spectre seen in lonely places, a melancholy portent. As the Bible said, the grass is green and all flesh is grass, waiting to be cut down by the reaper.

At Alloway there are also two splendid images of men at work: a smith shoeing a horse [see *fig.* 27], and a dyer at his dye tub. The setting up of an image valued the man, his trade and also the community which needed the tradesman. They are the first images of ordinary people to be put up in a typical Scottish country village. Sometimes the formal symbols of a trade were carved, like a hammer under a crown for a blacksmith. This was also painted on banners when the smiths walked in procession through the town, and, if they were wealthy enough to own a hall to meet in, over its door. Other trade symbols were the square and compasses for a wright, bakers' peels, a shuttle for a weaver, or scissors for a tailor. Rarely, objects for other occupations can be found, like the gun and fishing rod on the grave of a gamekeeper at New Galloway, or the compasses, axe and scraper commemorating a quaich-maker at Tranent. In these headstones the human race is starting to place itself in the middle of the stage of life, pushing away the witches and demons that had previously shared it.

There was also a growing appreciation of what really was exotic, as knowledge of other continents increased. Seamen brought rarities from distant ports, and there was a small trade in strange foods such as the pineapple. The *Scots Magazine* published articles about remarkable phenomena like the volcanoes in Iceland. Accounts of voyages and foreign lands were also popular, and there was sufficient demand for Admiral Anson's story of his voyage round the world to necessitate a reprint at Ayr in 1790. Unicorn's horns – actually narwhal tusk – were exhibited in London early in the eighteenth century, but by 1750 the unicorn was dead. The new enthusiasm for literal description had done for it.

One sign of the supernatural losing its terror was the appearance of spirits in children's games. 'Bogle about the stacks' was one example, a form of hide-and-seek. Jean Elliot's song 'The Flowers o' the Forest', first published in 1776, about the Scots who died at the Battle of Flodden, included the lines:

At e'en, in the gloaming, nae swankies are roaming [lively young men]
'Bout wi' the lassies at bogle to play.

1

1. Francis Grose FSA, *c.*1790

Steel engraving from an earlier portrait of the antiquary and friend of Robert Burns. The poet appreciated Grose's appetite for 'meikle glee and fun'.

(DUMFRIES MUSEUM)

2. 'Aloa Church, Airshire', 'deserted o' its riggin''

Copperplate engraving, 1790.

Burns wrote 'Tam o' Shanter' as a 'witch story' to accompany this illustration of Kirk Alloway, by Francis Grose in his *Antiquities of Scotland*, 1791.

(DUMFRIES MUSEUM)

2

3

3. Drumclog

Engraving from F. J. Child's *The English and Scottish Popular Ballads, c.*1898.

For those of Burns's generation, the bloody battles of the Covenanters were still vividly recalled. In this engraving an old man is using the memorial as a history lesson for the children.

(UNIVERSITY OF GLASGOW/ www.scran.ac.uk)

4. Stone in Auld Kirkyard, Ayr

The memorial stone to murdered Covenanters, *c.*1814, beside the Auld Kirk in Ayr where Burns worshipped as a boy. On the reverse of this stone are the lines:

'Boots, thumbikins were in fashion then / Lord never let us see such days again.'

(NATIONAL MUSEUMS SCOTLAND)

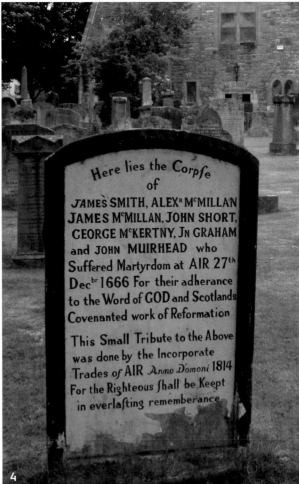

Here lies the Corpſe of JAMES SMITH, ALEXᴿ MᶜMILLAN JAMES MᶜMILLAN, JOHN SHORT, GEORGE MᶜKERTNY, Jᴺ GRAHAM and JOHN MUIRHEAD who Suffered Martyrdom at AIR 27ᵗʰ Decᵇʳ 1666 For their adherance to the Word of GOD and Scotlands Covenanted work of Reformation

This Small Tribute to the Above was done by the Incorporate Trades of AIR *Anno Domoni* 1814 For the Righteous ſhall be Kept in everlaſting rememberance

4

The Society of Scottish Antiquaries from the Editor

NEW EDITION,

WITH ADDITIONS BY BEETHOVEN & FRONTISPIECE BY WILKIE 1822.

A Select Collection of

ORIGINAL SCOTTISH AIRS

for the Voice.

With Introductory & Concluding Symphonies

& Accompaniments for the

PIANO FORTE, VIOLIN & VIOLONCELLO

By

Pleyel Kozeluch & Haydn

With

Select & Characteristic Verses both Scottish and English

Written for this Work by

BURNS &c.

THE WHOLE COLLECTED IN 5 VOLUMES BY G. THOMSON F.A.S.E.

Price of each Volume the Voice & Piano Forte One Guinea.
The Violin & Viol.lo parts separate 6.sh.

Now see where caledonia Genius mourns.
And plants the holly round the tomb of Burns.

Volume I. Ent.d at Stationers Hall. 1822

London, Printed & Sold by T. Preston 71 Dean S.t
Sold also by G. Thomson the Editor & Proprietor, Edinburgh.

G. Thomson

5. 'Original Scottish Airs for the Voice', 1822

Title page with dedication by George Thomson, the editor.

Thomson's alterations to many of the songs written by Burns for these volumes has led to criticism by some scholars, but the correspondence between the two shows a lively mutual respect. Thomson felt that the songs were equal to the best in Europe.

6. 'The Witches show Macbeth the Apparitions'

Circle of Alexander Runciman, c.1771-72.
Pen and brown ink over pencil on paper.

The powerful trio from 'Macbeth' add ingredients to
the cauldron in a list recalling the horrible details in
'Tam o' Shanter'.

7. 'The Jolly Beggars'

Engraving by S. Warren after
Sir William Allan RA, 1823.

A fig for those by law protected!
Liberty's a glorious feast!
Courts for cowards were erected,
Churches built to please the priest.
(Robert Burns)

(NATIONAL TRUST FOR SCOTLAND)

8. 'Weel done, Cutty-sark!'

Snuffbox of yellow varnished wood, by
G. Sliman of Catrine, Ayrshire, early 19th century.

Despite its small size, many of the gruesome
details from Tam o' Shanter are shown on the
lid. 'Auld Nick' himself, in the bottom right
corner, is very Scottish, wrapped in a plaid and
with a chieftain's feather in his bonnet.

(NATIONAL MUSEUMS SCOTLAND)

9. 'Kirkoswald and Tam o' Shanter's Grave', 1846

Steel engraving from a painting by D. O. Hill RSA.

The 16 year-old Burns learned surveying in one of the houses on the far side of the kirkyard. The fact that the font used for the christening of Robert Bruce was now in the kirkyard would have resonated with the poet's acute sense of history.

(DUMFRIES MUSEUM)

10. Communion tokens

A selection of Communion tokens from south-west Scotland, from Brook (1906-07).

Metal tokens were used as tickets of admission for the service of Holy Communion from late 16th to late 19th centuries. They often bear the parish name, date, and initials or name of the minister. Some of these drawings show both sides of the tokens. 'Anworth' [sic] has a bleeding heart and the initials of Robert Carson, minister. 'Machline' [sic] dates from the year 'Daddy' Auld became minister. The final image is a Covenanters' token.

(NATIONAL MUSEUMS SCOTLAND)

Anwoth

Mauchline

Tarbolton

10

Dumfries

Sanquhar

Kirkoswald

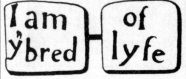

Covenanters' token

11. 'Tam o' Shanter'

Sepia drawing by John Faed, c.1850.

The 'hellish legion' in pursuit of Tam and Maggie, racing away from the light and into darkness.

During the 1850s Faed was commissioned by the Royal Association for the Promotion of Fine Arts in Scotland to illustrate Burns, including 'Tam o' Shanter' (1856).

(NATIONAL GALLERY OF SCOTLAND)

12. John Taylor (1703-72)

Engraved portrait of the 'quack' oculist who was often referred to as the 'Chevalier' Taylor, due to his particular success on the continent.

(EDINBURGH UNIVERSITY LIBRARY)

13. Headstone at Alloway

The skeletal Death snuffing out the candle of life on an 18th-century stone.

(NATIONAL MUSEUMS SCOTLAND)

14. Headstone at Alloway

The Green Man, a symbol of life and regeneration, rising from the earth on the headstone of Ivie Hair, who died in 1691.

(NATIONAL MUSEUMS SCOTLAND)

15. Map of the county of Wigton [*sic*], 1782

By John Ainslie, 1782, vignette detail.

The vignette emphasises the rich agriculture of the area, as well as trade. Exports on the left: goatskins and cheese. Imports on the right: barrels of wine and boxes of tea from China.

(NATIONAL LIBRARY OF SCOTLAND)

16. Receipt signed by Robert Burns, 1789

The poet is acknowledging payment by William Creech, an important Edinburgh bookseller and a founder member of the Society of Antiquaries of Scotland, for eighteen pounds and five shillings 'for Fifty Three Copies of my poems'.

Creech's overdue payment earned him this astringent portrait by Burns:

A little upright, pert, tart, tripping wight,
And still his precious Self his dear delight.

(NATIONAL MUSEUMS SCOTLAND)

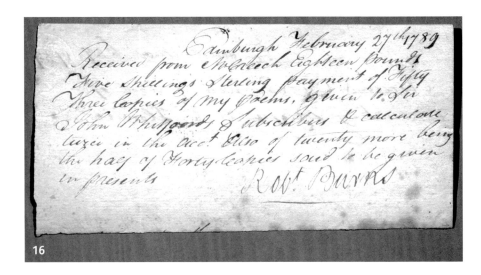

Ministers had once been seen as men of great spiritual power.

Them and their sessions, their cutty-stools, and full bottom'd wigs, hollow granes [groans], *and dranting prayers, made fowk at times almost swarf with dridder or dread.*

More than that, ministers had been able to interact with beings from other worlds, for they were 'creatures supernaturally endowed, fit to lay ghaists, talk with bogles and spreets, shake hands with death, and do many other such wonders'.[56]

Here is an example. James Borland, minister of the parish of Bedrule from 1690 to 1713, dealt with a changeling by feeding the thing a preparation from the flowers of the foxglove (known as the Devil's thimbles), and locking it in a barn overnight. When he opened the barn, the changeling had been replaced by the stolen child. In this period, too, ministers had sometimes been the ones who carried out the 'cut above the brow', or who 'scored abune the breath', to remove a witch's power. Ministers, however, had lost all these powers by Burns's time.

It was not just the belief in witches and other spirits that had disappeared; it was the whole world in which they had lived. They had brought a richness of meaning to the ways in which people saw the landscape and the beings that lived in it. The pattern of fashion, the market, the superficial, drove away the profound fears of the dark and the hunting, haunting owl. Now people had a greater awareness of the visual, but saw the superficial appearance rather than the emotional depth that lay below. In farmhouses in the evenings, tales about apparitions and fairies were told until the first decade of the nineteenth century, only to be replaced by conversation about 'the shortest and surest way to riches, or else consists of puerile scandal concerning absent lads and lassies'.[57] The *wag at the wa'* had once been an elf who sat on the cruik or fire-crane, and when he swung it to and fro it was a sign of bad luck. The label was soon to be applied to a German pendulum clock with a wooden mechanism, common in Dumfriesshire by 1790.[58]

NOTES

1   Robertson (1904), p. 2; Kinsley (1968), p. 558.
2   Hewat (1894), p. 99.
3   Cromek (1880), p. 220.
4   Edgar (1885-86), pp. 268-70.
5   Robertson (1904), p. 73; Kinsley (1968), p. 170.
6   Hogg (1807), p. 115.
7   *Scots Magazine*, May 1816, pp. 344-52.
8   Urquhart (2002).
9   Banks (1935).
10 Sullivan (1780), p. 222.
11 *Dumfries Weekly Journal*, 7 November 1826, 4b.
12 Johnstone (1867), pp. 21-22.
13 See Scott: *Guy Mannering*, ch. 3.
14 Fergusson (1807), p. 138.
15 *Ibid.*, p. 323.
16 Ferguson and Roy (1985), vol. 2, pp. 145-46.
17 *Ibid.*
18 Robertson (1904), p. 73; Kinsley (1968), p. 170.
19 Walker (1727), p. 94.
20 Robertson (1904), p. 73; Kinsley (1968), p. 171.
21 Irving (1816), p. 271.
22 Scot (1972), p. 86.
23 *Edinburgh Magazine*, January 1819, 219-24.
24 Child (1882-98), vol. 1, pp. 335-58.
25 *Old Statistical Account*: Closeburn.
26 Pennant (1771), pp. 94-95.
27 MacTaggart (1824), p. 210.
28 *Alchemilla vulgaris*.
29 Henderson (1812), p. 204, quoted by Black (1892-93), p. 466.
30 Evans (1872), quoted by Black (1892-93), p. 467.
31 Ferguson and Roy (1985), vol. 2, pp. 145-46.
32 A. M. (1820).
33 Wilson (1904), pp. 51-55.
34 A. M. (1820).
35 *Ibid.*
36 *Ibid.*
37 *Ibid.*
38 Robertson (1904), p. 103; Kinsley (1968), p. 440.
39 *Ibid.* (1904), p. 66; (1968), p. 83.
40 Ferguson and Roy (1985), vol. 1, p. 135.
41 *Scots Magazine* (1816), p. 347.
42 MacTaggart (1824), p. 25-30.
43 Mure (1854), p. 266.
44 *Ibid.*, p. 269.
45 Johnson (1775), p. 252.
46 Dick (1972), p. 36.
47 *OSA*: Wigtown.
48 Robertson (1904), p. 25; Kinsley (1968), p. 162.
49 *Ibid.* (1904), p. 72; (1968), p. 169.
50 MacTaggart (1824), p. 277.
51 *OSA*: Closeburn.
52 Quoted by Thin (1938), p. 142.
53 Riddell (1792), p. 15.
54 Ferguson and Roy (1985), vol. 2, p. 93.
55 Roy (1777), p. 654.
56 MacTaggart (1824), p. 386.
57 *Scots Magazine* (1818), p. 153.
58 *OSA*: Kirkpatrick-Juxta.

CHAPTER 5

Evil Men, Bad Weather
and the Awful Future

But oh! I backward cast my e'e,
On prospects drear!
An' forward, tho' I canna see,
I guess an' fear![1]

BURNS wrote these lines in a gloomy moment. The world was full of predators, like lawyers and roof-lifting storms that destroyed crops. Life was not always pleasant, and early death and lingering poverty were common: 'There's nocht but care on every hand.' The farmer was at the mercy of the weather, as were the cottar's potato patch and the shepherd's flock. Violent crime was rare but shocking. There were many threats to a stable life, many sources of uncertainty. One was the witch who performed disruptive acts and also brought storms. And underlying it all was the frailty of humankind, for by breaking the covenant, Adam and Eve had introduced sin. The Devil, 'laying hold of this instrument [the human race], his kingdom has made great progress in the world,' wrote William Burnes.[2]

One local figure, executed a century and a half before Burns was born, was starkly nasty: John Mure of Auchendrane.[3] The towerhouse of Auchendrane was over the shoulder of the hill south of Alloway, by the tightly-winding Doon in its cleft of a valley, with sharp little glens running down from the lumpy Carrick hills: a pattern of shadows, with foxes padding through it. Mure was active in the reign of James VI, when blood feuds ran through meshes of greed and personal ill-feeling, and through the visceral wish to grasp and hold land. These were slow-stewing loathings, with long silences in which men tended their anger, tempered swords and put an edge to their blades, and the plot of each enmity moved death by death. In this world Auchendrane was a great talent, spinning out words of insincere friendship, lying about family ties, and waiting for the moment to strike. He murdered and encouraged others to do so.

It was Mure, then in his seventies, who persuaded the young Gilbert Kennedy of Bargany to ride home from Ayr, through Alloway and over the Brig o' Doon, when he knew that his kinsman Sir Thomas Kennedy was out with 200 horsemen, hoping to intercept Gilbert and kill him, which he did.

Bargany's family had a 'banner of revenge' made. The first of these had been for the murder in Edinburgh of Mary Queen of Scots's husband, Henry Stewart, Earl of Darnley, in 1567. This memorial was painted in London, and shows Darnley lying dead on his tomb, his parents and brother praying beside him, and in front his infant son King James VI. As Dr Duncan Thomson put it, 'it can be read as a mounting wail of despair for the death of a son and a deafening call for revenge'.[4] A generation later, King James himself was implicated in the slaying by the Catholic Earl of Huntly of the ultra-Protestant James Stewart (c.1568-92), Earl of Moray, at Donibristle on the coast of Fife. A banner was painted with the text, 'GOD REVENGE MY CAUS'. It is horrifyingly realistic, showing two sword cuts across the right side of Moray's face, a huge cut in his right thigh that must have gone to the bone, and half a dozen puncture wounds in his chest and belly. Bargany's banner does not survive, but it seems to have been similar. It bore a painting of the dead man, showing his wounds, his son sitting at his knees, with the words 'Judge and Rewendge my caus, O Lord'.[5]

The events that led up to John Mure's death show the lengths to which he would go to seek advantage. His near relative and supposed friend, Kennedy of Colzean, sent a message to Mure saying that he would be passing through Ayr on the way to Edinburgh, asking if there were letters or anything else he could carry to the capital. The message was carried by a boy named William Dalrymple, and Mure instructed him to return to Colzean and tell him he had not been able to deliver the message. Mure had the unaware Colzean murdered on the road between

Alloway and Ayr. Then Dalrymple had to be kept silent, so Mure locked him up before sending him to the island of Arran. Dalrymple, however, escaped and reached the mainland, and was induced to go to the Low Countries as a soldier. Five years later he re-emerged, seemingly trying to blackmail Mure: he cannot have understood what a force he was dealing with. Mure and his son met Dalrymple on the beach at Girvan and suffocated him by holding him face-down in the sand. The corpse was allowed to drift out to sea, and when the tide brought it back to land it was taken for a seafarer and buried. When it was exhumed and identified later, the Mures were taken to Edinburgh, justice, and the maiden (later called the guillotine).

These events were known to the people of southern Ayrshire and particularly to those living where the drama had been performed. Criminal acts were not the stuff of distant legend, but real violence done by real people, and the families of the killers and victims were still living in the area.

More recent crimes were evident when Burns was a boy. David Edwards was an English soldier who in 1758 murdered the regimental shoemaker. Executed on Ayr Common, his bones were left to hang in the gibbet, the chains and gibbet-irons rattling and ringing from time to time and echoing in the mind of the poet.[6]

A murder took place two miles from Alloway after the Burns family had moved to Mount Oliphant. In 1771 Marjorie Williamson was walking towards Ochiltree after the Ayr Midsummer fair. She and her husband had become separated, but they met on the road and argued, and then he threw her over a 'high precipice' into a mill-dam before beating her with the big end of his whip. Her body was found 'among some whins', but her husband disappeared: there was no trial and so no formal record.[7]

There had also been a murder connected with Mossgiel. Long before Burns arrived there, Mungo Campbell had been the tenant. In 1642 he killed his cousin John Campbell in Mauchline: why or how is not known. These were troubled times – Royalist forces had lately been defeated by the Covenanters, and civil war was breaking out in England. Campbell's case was handled not by civil law but through a church court, the Presbytery of Ayr. He was sentenced to appear in Mauchline kirk twice, and at half-a-dozen nearby parishes on following Sundays, dressed in sackcloth.[8]

Robert Carson, minister of Anwoth (d.1769), was a quite different kind of sinner. He had a remote parish on the coast of the Solway Firth. Seven elders raised a petition claiming that he was guilty of first, smuggling, and encouraging smuggling; second, cursing and swearing; third, lying and dissimulation; fourth, 'obscene discourse'; fifth, 'advising to commit immoral behaviour'; sixth, scoffing at sacred things; and seventh and finally, forging writs.[9] To say the least, he was at odds with his kirk session. His case was heard in Edinburgh by the General Assembly: all Scotland knew that he had been deposed from his parish.

These crimes related to the supernatural because they could be seen as the result of the work of the Devil, who had encouraged the greed and hatred in which they had their roots. And Satan was more than a spectator at acts of evil. He was the proprietor of Hell, where he expected to receive the criminals in due time. In addition, the ghosts of victims might appear on earth to seek redress for their sufferings.

Dreams were on the border of the supernatural, and were a way in which information might be revealed. Sometimes they provided helpful information which enabled the detection of crime or the finding of lost objects. For example, in 1707 John Strachan of Craigcrook, who lived just west of Edinburgh, had two servants. The woman servant was prudent and saved her money; the man servant killed her, stole her savings, left the family's employment, and set up as a smith. Craigcrook's wife dreamed that the manservant was the murderer, and that he had hidden the money in barrels which appeared to be full of nails. When his premises were searched, the money was found as predicted: confession and execution followed.[10]

Dreams, however, were not admissible as evidence in a trial. At the High Court of Justiciary in 1754 two men were charged with murder. Alexander Macpherson gave evidence that in the summer of 1750, when he was 20 years old and living on a shieling near Braemar, a figure came to his bedside in the night and took him to a peat moss to indicate the spot where Macpherson next day found a body. He left the corpse where it was found and the figure appeared again to ask him to bury it. The body was that of Sergeant Arthur Davies who had disappeared the previous year, and he named his murderers. Macpherson's story was taken sufficiently seriously for more prosaic evidence to be sought, but neither the word of the ghost, nor the loosely circumstantial evidence which had been found, could secure a conviction.[11]

Popular belief in the supernatural could be useful to smugglers, who were night birds and capable of inventing stories. Sometimes they moved their contraband silently on men's backs. To cover other methods, tales were told of teams of horses without a driver, pulling loads around midnight. These ghostly horses were said to strike out with their hooves with perfect accuracy if someone tried to stop them.[12]

The memory of the Covenanting period of the late seventeenth century was an important part of popular culture, particularly in southwest Scotland. It included a sense of having been cruelly wronged by evil oppressors. The Covenanters sought religious liberty, and were still seen as fighters for freedom in Burns's time. Torture had been used to extract information from them, and a stone in the Auld Kirkyard at Ayr, still standing, says: 'Boots, thumbikins [thumb screws] were in fashion then / Lord never let us see such days again' [see *fig. 4*]. Boots were iron cases put over the feet and lower leg: wedges were driven into them to crush the bones.

At Balmaghie, in the midst of the hills, Burns wrote:

The Solemn League and Covenant
Now brings a smile, now brings a tear;
But sacred Freedom, too, was theirs:
If thou'rt a slave, indulge thy sneer.[13]

The Auld Lichts wing of the Kirk were their descendants, with the same dramatic and uncompromising belief in Hell.

The Covenanters were outdoor people, worshipping in the landscape. Their meeting places were in the hills, and they hid in upland glens. Such a place was the Whig's hole, a depression in the ground halfway up a hillside, where the Covenanters could wait, invisible from below. Their largest meetings were held on hill-tops. The one on Craigdow, south of Maybole, in 1677 drew 8000 people to a place which looked westwards out to sea, north to the farming land of Kyle, and south to the rough, high ground of Galloway, a nearby fastness. 'Prophet' Peden baptised children in the Glenmuir Water – the name only hints at the rough, tussocky remoteness of the place. The spot he chose was at the meeting of two waters, at the foot of a waterfall. Battles were commemorated by services on their sites, like Drumclog [see *fig. 3*] and Bothwell Bridge (both 1679), and individuals were buried where they were struck down. Over the Galloway hills are their resting places, 'Grey recumbent tombs of the dead in desert places, / Standing stones on the vacant wine-red moor', as Robert Louis Stevenson put it.[14]

The most violent phase in Covenanting had been in the 1680s, and it was still a living topic of conversation in Burns's time. Walter Scott described a leader on the government side, Robert Redgauntlet (his name shows that he had blood on his hands), who was in reality the bold figure of Robert Grierson of Lag:

> ... he came down here, rampauging like a lion, with commission of lieutenancy (and of lunacy, for what I ken), to put down a' the Whigs and Covenanters in the country. Wild wark they made of it; for the Whigs were as dour as the Cavaliers were fierce, and it was which should first tire the other. Redgauntlet was aye for the strong hand; and his name is kend as wide in the country as Claverhouse's or Tam Dalyell's. Glen, nor dargle, nor mountain, nor cave could hide the puir hill-folk when Redgauntlet was out with bugle and blood-hound after them, as if they had been sae mony deer. And, troth, when they fand them, they didna make muckle mair ceremony than a Hielandman wi' a roebuck. It was just, 'Will ye tak' the test?' If not—'Make ready–present–fire!' and there lay the recusant.[15]

The 'test' was to accept the Test Act of 1681 which enforced the rule of bishops in the Church of Scotland. It was disliked by much of the Kirk and loathed by the Covenanters.

Lag was cruel and efficient.[16] In February 1685 he had two men hanged at Irongray and five shot at Anwoth: like the old saying, 'a gloved cat was never a good hunter'. People assumed that he was in league with the Devil: a sign was that the Devil's mark, a horseshoe, appeared on his forehead when he was excited. And how, other than by calling upon the supernatural, are we to understand the story of the death of Grierson of Lag? On the last day of the year, men on ships in the Solway saw a coach and horses travelling over the waves in a violent storm, to collect for the Devil the soul of Lag who lay dying at Dumfries. On the day of the funeral, the horses could not move his hearse because they were held by a supernatural force. A fine pair from Spain – with the implication of some Catholic involvement – were harnessed instead, and they took off at a gallop to the kirkyard at Dunscore and dropped dead when they arrived.[17] When Burns lived at Ellisland he was half a mile from Lag's grave.

The Black Horseman was a Galloway ghost, said to have been a Danish king: he made his appearances on his huge steed at a ford in the middle of the big hills. A farmer's son called George McMillan, with his sister riding pillion, saw him in 1809 and galloped after him up a hill, watching the horseman until he faded away in the west. What is significant is that despite being dressed as an early medieval warrior, people said that he had been killed by Grierson of Lag.

In the south-west it was still common in the 1840s to have someone 'play Lag' on an evening in early November, newly dark and windy enough to make trees groan and windows rattle. A member of the company dressed up 'in shape of beast as hideous as ingenuity of the performer intrusted with the part could make it'. In one family, a servant, Margaret Edgar, drew a blanket round herself and over her head so that only hands and feet were visible:

> The kitchen implement called in Scotland a 'potato beetle,' which is a large wooden pestle, with handle pretty thick, and between two and three feet long, ending in a ponderous oval head, was entirely covered with strips of cloth being wrapped round it; eyes were drawn upon it, and pieces of fur sewed on for eyebrows; long ears and a mouth were added, the long handle of the instrument forming an imposing proboscis. The structure was fastened to the head of the performer, who moved on hands and knees, the result was a quadruped resembling ... the tapir of Borneo.[18]

After dinner most of the lights were dowsed, and

> ... a moaning most melancholy is heard, and anon the door is slowly opened and the end of the hag's long nose appears, then the glowing eyes and long ears of the creature, who proceeds, with stealthy steps and head on one side, to listen for sounds of a home-conventicle, and to smell out Covenanters under the sideboard.[19]

Lag had lost all his power, and was no more than an entertainment for children – but he was still there.

The Covenanters continued superstitions, such as placing a small silver coin under heels of those being married, to prevent the Devil from interfering with the happiness of the marriage.[20] They also looked for supernatural signs. There is a story that a communion cup which had belonged to John MacMillan, one of the leaders of the spiritual descendents of the Covenanters, was used to make a test of an individual's belief. If someone trembled when they took it, or otherwise seemed agitated, then they were not pure Calvinists.

The Covenanters read the Bible as literal truth, and their hunting by government forces was as stern and swift as an Old Testament story. Yet when these persecutors themselves suffered, it was often in a time and manner which makes one think that the mysterious force of providence was at work. Sir John Cochrane, whose niece married Claverhouse, informed the military about the hiding place of the preacher Richard Cameron. With some hard riding and swords clashing in a skirmish, the Covenanting preacher was soon a corpse. Cochrane's house burned down shortly after. All over the south-west the extinction of great families and the dilapidation of their mansions were seen as signs of providence, and were 'rehearsed with solemn emphasis around the evening fire'.

A church in upper Nithsdale lost its weekly purpose when the tiny parish of Kirkbride was divided between two others. In the suppression of the parish, one aim was the removal of a secluded meeting place for Covenanters. Abraham Crichton of Sanquhar sent workmen to 'ding dune the Whigs' sanctuary', though one might guess that he had a use for good building stone. The men were driven off by a storm, and later Crichton fell from his horse and was killed. His angry ghost was seen thereabouts for years. This was about 1750, when it was still the practice for dairy maids to take their pails into the fields to milk the cows. The ghost's interventions caused screams, scampering over the grass and spilt milk.[21]

In the hills between Ayrshire and Dumfries, two Covenanters, 'the martyrs of Cairn', were shot and buried where they fell. A large flat stone was placed near the grave, but a farmer took it and laid it on the clay floor in front of his fire. Soon it shattered into a hundred pieces.[22] Another story was set on the edge of the Ayrshire moors, where John McGeaghan was wounded in an attack on troops which freed a minister. The dying man, making his way home, called at a farmhouse for help, but he was turned away without even a cup of milk or water. They say cattle pastured there would not give milk thereafter, and more than a century later the farmer did not keep cattle.

Stories of providence were told not only of Covenanters. The model for Madge Wildfire in Walter Scott's *The Heart of Midlothian* (1818), for example, was a shepherdess who wandered with her flock over Ayrshire, Galloway, and beyond, for six years from 1769. She was said to have fallen in love with a shepherd near Bristol, but her father deemed the man unsuitable and shot him. As the man lay dying, he gave her the animals. Later her favourite ram, Charlie, was killed after he wandered into a kailyard and the farmer set a mastiff on him. Shortly after, the farmer was nearly drowned in a peat hag; and when a butcher in Kilmarnock struck one of her sheep, his hand withered.[23]

Thus far this chapter has looked at great crimes – actions which involve a degree of evil which is difficult to explain in terms of familiar levels of emotion so that they seemed to have about them something beyond this normal world. We can now move on to a more human level, to people whose chief crime is to stand outside conventional life. Some would say that they break laws and commandments, but in reality they ignore them.

> A fig for those by law protected!
> Liberty's a glorious feast!
> Courts for Cowards were erected,
> Churches built to please the Priest!

Burns's 'The Jolly Beggars', according to Professor David Daiches, is a remarkable anarchist cantata [fig. 7]. To use Burns's own phrase, its cast is a group of 'gangrel bodies', beggars and other opportunists. They included a soldier who had lost a leg and an arm, and is now a beggar, and his female partner. He says:

> My 'prenticeship I pass'd where my leader breath'd his last,
> When the bloody die was cast on the heights of Abram.[24]

He is saying that he had been with General Wolfe at Quebec in 1759, and implying that the risks he took entitle him to a life of ease. There is also an acrobat, a widow who is a thief – she has 'no comfort but a hearty can' – a fiddler, a tinker and a poet. The members of this group are loyal to one another. Part of their method is to wait for days like harvest festivals or *kirns*:

> At kirns an' weddings we'se be there,
> And oh! sae nicely's we will fare;
> We'll bouse about, till Daddie Care
> Sings whistle owre the lave o't.[25]

At these events, people would be celebrating and likely to be free with their money, particularly if drunk.

Groups like this did exist. According to the *Scots Magazine*, 'A banditti of eight vagrants' met a man who had just found £1600 lying on a road in Fife. (The story is only credible if we assume that these are pounds Scots, one twelfth of the value of pounds sterling.) They took most of it and headed south. At Penrith they spent £160 on 'millinery goods' and other finery, and were captured at Preston 'making merry over a large bowl of punch'.[26] They had attracted attention because they never used any small change. Did this actually happen? Who knows? And perhaps it does not matter. The story nonetheless reveals the fear of itinerants who lived without much interest in law or convention. They knew, as the Auld Lichts did not, how to enjoy themselves.

The aim of a band like the Jolly Beggars was to make a living without working. Burns associates them with two virtues: freedom of action, and the belief that possessions are less important than people. He sees the poet as being the same kind of outsider, another 'gangrel body':

> *He had nae wish, but to be glad,*
> *Nor want but when he thirsted;*
> *He hated nought but to be sad,*
> *And thus the Muse suggested*
> *His sang that night.*[27]

In each parish the organisation of the public affairs of the kirk were in the hands of the kirk session, including provision for the poor, for education, and arrangements for the burial of the dead. The session was made up of male parishioners selected for their piety and common sense. These elders were administrators, and the session a minor court before which those suspected of misdemeanours could be called to explain themselves. Elders visited races and fairs to observe behaviour, and under the name of 'civillisers' they went to alehouses between 9 and 10 o'clock at night to disperse drinkers. These elders were not themselves perfect, however. One was brought before Mauchline kirk session for fighting: on the night of the February fair he had ejected a man from a public house and the situation got out of hand. Punishment centred on public censure by the minister in church, and this was sometimes strongly worded: 'gentle admonitions touch only gentle minds, and where there is a hard hide there needs to be a sharp censure.'[28] In the seventeenth century, miscreants had been obliged to wear sackcloth before the congregation, and a new gown of sackcloth was bought by Mauchline kirk session in 1748 and used as late as 1781.[29]

The staples of the session's activity were petty crime, domestic violence and minor immorality. Thus in Mauchline in 1773 it dealt with the case of a woman who wounded her mother-in-law with fire tongs. Four years later it dealt with Kitran [Katherine] Angus who 'threatened to stick Robert Gibb' with a *graip* [a fork]. She replied that if she had a graip, he had a flail.[30] Theft took place, but it was rarely more than some coal, a hive of bees, or a hen.[31] And Burns put into the mouth of one member of the Mauchline Session, 'Holy Willie', the assertion that Burns's friend Gavin Hamilton was a sinner because he 'drinks, an' swears, an' plays at cartes'.

Just as crime was caused by evil, bad weather – the storm which ruined the crops, the frost which blighted the buds, the spate which drowned the sheep – might have its root in evil too. Adverse weather systems may well be the deliberate actions of a witch, if they were not God's judgement on the errant human race.

Poor years and bad seasons were remembered for a century: they showed an ever-present threat to the farming on which everyone depended. For example, the summer and harvest of 1739 were very wet. On 20 May 1740 the frost was so intense that people could not cast their peats. In contrast, the 1750s and 1760s were warm and sometimes so dry that stock grazing out on the Dumfriesshire hills died of thirst.[32]

A sharper fear stemmed from the sudden danger caused by extremes of weather. Burns describes the effect of day-long rain coming after a heavy snowfall in 'The Brigs of Ayr':

> *Arous'd by blust'ring winds an' spotting thowes,*
> *In mony a torrent down the snaw-broo rowes;*
> *While crashing ice, borne on the roaring spate,*
> *Sweeps dams, an' mills, an' brigs, a' to the gate;*
> *And from Glenbuck, down to the Ratton-key,*
> *Auld Ayr is just one lengthen'd, tumbling sea.*[33]

There is both a personal and a general point to be found in the report in the Dumfries newspaper in March 1789 that 'a few days ago a man travelling between Port William and Glenluce, unfortunately perished in the late fall of snow. He had an old brown suit of clothes, and a basket in his hand, and is supposed to come from Dumfries.'[34] This is the individual tragedy of a man dying alone and unknown in the snow. But out there in the cold, it could happen to anyone: 'in the snaw the chapman smoor'd' [was smothered].

In other Dumfries newspapers of Burns's period we can find stories like the flood which lifted newly cut corn from the fields along the Nith. A storm in January 1794 uprooted trees, and tore roofs from houses. Four shepherds were buried in the snow at Moffat, said a report, eleven more were missing, and many sheep died. In the same storm, three men were drowned in Kirkcudbright. The destruction was greatest in Eskdale parish, where 4000 sheep died; and on the Beds of Esk, a sandbank at the head of the Solway Firth, lay the corpses of a woman, two men, three horses, nine cattle, 45 dogs (most of them presumably sheepdogs), 1800 sheep and 180 hares.[35]

Events like this were so dramatic that they demanded explanation. Perhaps it was the hand of God? Or had the Devil caused the storm and flood, either directly or through witches? Increasingly though, men with an interest in the natural world – who in the nineteenth century would be called scientists – suggested explanations based on things they could see.

John Pringle (1707-82), son of a Border laird, educated in medicine at Leyden and Paris, had been Physician-General to the Army and moved in the highest professional, intellectual and social circles. He was with the Duke of Cumberland at Culloden and became Physician to the king. Pringle engaged in important debates such as the nature of different fevers and the design of lightning conductors (he favoured pointed rather than blunt ones, and he lost his place at court because his opinion was the opposite to the king's). When a spectacular meteor shot across the British Isles in November 1758, Pringle was in practice in London and well-connected in scientific circles. He made a study of the meteor by asking about 20 people to collect information for him. They were all over Britain, and most were either surgeons or physicians. One was Dr Gilchrist of Dumfries, and another Lord Auchinleck, the father of James Boswell whose estate was near Mauchline. In each case, Pringle set out what he had been told and how much weight he put behind that piece of evidence. He concluded that over Cambridge the meteor had been about 100 miles high, but only 30 when it passed over Fort William.[36]

Pringle's family had land at Stichill on the Tweed. Ten miles to the east was the little estate of Patrick Brydone, who was so interested in lightning and other electrical effects in the atmosphere that he spent time studying them in the Alps. Burns took tea with Brydone in May 1787 at his home near Coldstream and listened as Brydone described a bizarre and exciting event when a cart of coal coming up from the River Tweed was at the centre of an enormous electrical discharge,[37] and the two horses and the driver were killed. Brydone described the driver, his body livid, his right leg shrivelled, clothes torn to pieces, a strong smell of burning, his hair and hat fused together. Brydone even sent the hat to London to be examined. He also interviewed lots of witnesses and people who had experienced strange effects around the same time. The event may have been extraordinary, but Brydone sought an explanation based on facts that could be demonstrated.

The *Scots Magazine* recounted what happened at Kirkconnel House (south-west of Dumfries), the home of Burns's friend William Maxwell. In 1783 it was struck by lightning, and the electricity, as it fizzled down the stone staircase to the ground floor, set the bells ringing, melted the bell wires leaving the ceilings blackened, and shattered an iron grate in a fireplace in a bedroom.[38] There was no suggestion in this of the supernatural. The point was how *extraordinary* nature could be.

In 1783 and the years after, a cloud covered western Europe, blighting crops. From Scotland the Sun looked as though 'a crust of heated iron' was 'over his burning disk … the husky, hot and stifling fog had withered and scorched the earth'.[39]

It was caused by the eruption of a volcano in Iceland. Some people believed it was the approach of the Day of Judgement.

NOTES

1 Robertson (1904), p. 110; Kinsley (1968), p. 128.
2 Burnes (1875), p. xl.
3 Paterson (1863-66), vol. 2, p. 404.
4 Thomson (1975), p. 19.
5 Paterson (1863-66), vol. 2, p. 404.
6 Young (1998), pp. 1, 47.
7 *Scots Magazine*, 33 (1771), 496.
8 Edgar (1885-86), pp. 248-51.
9 *Scots Magazine*, 29 (1767), p. 332.
10 Wodrow (1842-43), vol. 4, p. 172.
11 *Scots Magazine*, June 1754.
12 Steven (1899), p.94.
13 Robertson (1904), p. 292; Kinsley (1968), p. 803.
14 Stevenson (1950), p. 284.
15 Scott (1824), letter xl.
16 Fergusson (1886), pp. 29-62.
17 *Ibid.*, pp. 144-49.
18 *Ibid.*, pp. 7-9.
19 *Ibid.*, p. 8.
20 Stevenson (1880-81), p. 139n.
21 Wilson (1904), p. 29.
22 Steven (1899), p. 52.
23 *Ibid.*, pp. 99-105.

24 Robertson (1904), p. 8; Kinsley (1968), p. 196.
25 *Ibid.* (1904), p. 12; (1968), p. 203.
26 *Scots Magazine*, 48 (1786), p. 567.
27 Robertson (1904), p. 14; Kinsley (1968), p. 205.
28 Edgar (1885), p. 199.
29 *Ibid.*, p. 293.
30 *Ibid.*, pp. 246-47.
31 *Ibid.*, pp. 247-48.
32 *Old Statistical Account*: Eskdalemuir; Lamb (1982), p. 236.
33 Robertson (1904), p. 48; Kinsley (1968), p. 286.
34 *Dumfries Weekly Journal*, 24 March 1789, 4a.
35 Hogg (1995), p. 5.
36 Pringle (1759-60).
37 *Scots Magazine*, 49 (1787), p. 313.
38 *Ibid.*, 45 (1783), p. 390.
39 *Edinburgh Magazine*, February 1822, p. 188.

CHAPTER 6

Medicines

HEALTH is a continuing interest for all human beings: their own health, and that of their family and neighbours. On an Ayrshire farm, good health meant being able to work the day round, and someone sick was a consumer of food who contributed no work for the common good. Some illnesses were slow, undermining the frame, like the tuberculosis which consumed William Burnes. Other infirmities came from minor accidents whose results, untreated, lessened the labouring effectiveness of the strong, and underfeeding laid the poor open to a range of diseases. Death in childhood threatened the survival of the family. Robert Burns and Jean Armour had nine children: four died before they were four years old, and Frances Wallace Burns when she was 14. People wanted hope.

Some aspects of health were straightforward matters of observation, open to anyone who could weigh up the evidence to hand. Thus the fact that Kilmarnock remained healthy when there were epidemics of fever in Ayr and Irvine was explained by the latter towns being seaports.[1] Similarly, it was understood that fevers were introduced to country districts by servants who had moved from a town. People also observed that families living at a distance from one another contributed to healthiness at a time when infectious diseases were common and often fatal. It was recognised that there were certain things which one could do to maintain health, such as eating well and taking exercise, and that amiable sociability was good for the mind and therefore good for the body. In one Ayrshire parish the basis for wellbeing was that 'the inhabitants of both town and country enjoy the comforts of society ... in superior degree to others in similar conditions of life'.[2]

One aspect of practical medicine – inoculation – was controversial. The practice had been introduced from Asia, via the Middle East, to Britain in the 1720s. The idea of making a child ill as a protection against smallpox was odd, and many condemned it as the impious distrust of divine providence.[3] It was also dangerous because it involved an attack of smallpox, which might be fatal, and not cowpox, a much less dangerous disease (introduced later by Edward Jenner). Dumfries was one place where smallpox inoculation was favoured: more than 100 people had died there in an epidemic in 1734, and the risk was seen as being acceptable. The threat of another epidemic in 1789 was met with a 'general inoculation'.[4]

In retrospect the power of medicine was limited by lack of knowledge. There were many errors of judgement. The minister of Kirkoswald, for example, thought that fevers were less severe there because tea and sugar were widely used. His colleague at Gretna, however, condemned the 'indiscriminate use of tea' as damaging to health. People saw patterns that shaped the way they looked at health and sickness. The wife of Anthony Shaw of Glasgow, for instance, had a bleeding nose. By tradition and family experience – her father and husband had died after their noses bled – she knew her end was near. She asked her daughter which room she should pass away in, moved into the front room of her house, and in three or four days expired.[5] John Peadie of Roughhill died in 1731 from a natural cause, inflammation of the lungs. Three years earlier his father had been walking through the trees beside the house when an owl had flown across his path in one direction, and then the other. Within a month his father was dead, and when John saw an owl fly in the same way, he expected his own demise. And so it was.[6]

A central concern was the quality of the air. The sea air at Ayr was healthy: 'No fields can be more commodious for walking, or the healthful exercises of riding and golfing.'[7] The air was always damper near to water, and building houses on a riverbank was seen as a way of damaging health if not actively promoting disease. The better drainage brought by ditches along the fields, however, removed stagnant water and made the country healthier.[8]

Physicians were the educated élite of the medical world, trained at university to understand the balances which had to be maintained in a healthy human body. But they were the few. When Burns was an adult there were one or two physicians in each of the larger towns such as Kilmarnock, Ayr, Irvine and Dumfries. Their professional services were costly, for they were the social equals of the merchants and all but the most opulent of the lairds whom they treated. The one whom Burns knew best in his early years was John Mackenzie, who practised in Mauchline and attended William Burnes when he was dying. Mackenzie later moved to the burgh of Irvine where he was paid a retainer of £100 a year by the Earl of Eglinton to keep him at hand.

One sign that Robert was rising in the world was his friendship with the physician James Adair. Burns made a trip from Edinburgh to Clackmannan with Adair, where the latter met the woman who was to become his wife – Charlotte, half-sister of Gavin Hamilton of Mauchline, the lawyer to whom Burns had dedicated the Kilmarnock edition.

The basis for the medicine of learned men and patients who could afford it was the idea of balance. 'Live in measure,' said the proverb, 'and laugh at the mediciners.' On this basis, fevers and rheumatisms were seen as being caused by exposure to variable weather, cooling peoples' bodies suddenly 'when warmed with their labour'. Fever was also caused by wearing wet clothes and living in damp houses – but how else could a cotter or farm labourer live?[9] The physicians' cures were slow and thoughtful. The tired professional man, or laird who was strained by his responsibilities, might be sent to the countryside to drinks goats' whey. This pungent substance strengthened his constitution, while fresh air and exercise – horse riding, perhaps, or fishing – built him up for another year's activity.[10]

There was a moral flavour to this idea of balance. In the 'Address to the Unco Guid', Burns said:

> Who made the heart, 'tis He alone
> Decidedly can try us;
> He knows each chord, its various tone,
> Each spring, its various bias.[11]

God was the judge of the balances in the life of a human being, the cruelties and kindnesses, the thoughtfulness and selfishness. The physician had a similar role with regard to the body. More broadly, anything surprising was an indication that there was an imbalance in the cosmos, even if the event appeared to be positive. A more than usually fine crop was a *fey-crap*, and it indicated the death of the farmer: the world operated on a zero-sum basis, and good had to be balanced by evil.

Compared with physicians, there was a larger number of surgeons, who were more concerned with problems on the outside of the body, or which were otherwise evident to the sight: broken bones, strains, gashes, and the effects of accidents. In the cities some of these men were full-time surgeons, like 'Lang' Sandy Wood who treated Burns when he dislocated his knee-cap. The physician had the status of a professional man and so could not be seen to be making money from the trade in medicines, but the surgeon was not thus constrained. Most outside the cities were surgeon-apothecaries, who sold medicines and dispensed a wide range of medical advice. They were thus general practitioners in all but name, and they were able to advertise their services, drugs and prepared medicines they sold. In Dumfries, surgeon-apothecaries stocked bottled water from Hartfell Spa at the head of Annandale, and from Bad Pyrmont in Germany[12] (Burns called it 'drumlie [muddy] German-water'). William Inglis, surgeon in Dumfries, sold honey.[13]

Surgeons also practised in smaller towns and in a few country parishes, living in one and serving several. The practice of the surgeon in the Nithsdale parish of Morton 'extends for a large district of country around', the same area in which Burns the exciseman was travelling from Ellisland, a few miles down the valley.[14] In Ballantrae, on the then remote south Ayrshire coast, there was 'no surgeon or physician within half a dozen miles, and it is doubtful whether half a dozen such parishes will give bread to one'.[15]

It is also possible that ministers and their wives provided medical help within their parishes. The minister's wife was almost the only person in the parish likely to own a recipe book. This was normally a handwritten book that contained instructions for making various dishes, but would have notes on the use of herbs to gain and sustain health.[16] Hugh Thomson of Kilmaurs was an unusual example. Having been a successful physician, he took the cloth, and gave medical advice to his parishioners without payment. His son, however, sold the medicines his father had specified.[17]

The most common treatment was to do nothing and let nature take its course. This was the fatalism of subsistence farming, an attitude not just to human health but to weather and the growth of crops. It was also fatalism in the face of the inevitable. 'But death, against whom there is no defence, is ever snatching some of all ranks and ages, the rich and the poor, the young and the healthy, as well as the old and the diseased,' wrote William Auld of Mauchline.[18] This was conventional thought and language. Robert Fergusson spoke of the poor more poignantly:

> *No doctor need their weary life to spae,* [predict]
> *Nor drogs their noddle and their sense confound,*
> *Till death slip sleely on, and gi'e the hindmost wound.*[19]

'Late crippled of an arm, and now a leg' – suffering from a dislocated knee-cap, and laid up in bed – Burns wrote to his patron Robert Graham of Fintry about the psychological effect of immobility. Burns was 'dull, listless, teas'd, dejected, and deprest'. In this mood, he compared the animal and the human world:

> *Foxes and statesmen, subtle wiles ensure;*
> *The cit and the polecat stink, and are secure.* [citizen]
> *Toads with their poison, doctors with their drug,*
> *The priest and hedgehog in their robes, are snug.*[20]

From this Burns moves on to writers' favourite catharsis, the attack on critics:

> *Critics – appall'd I venture on the name,*
> *Those cut-throat bandits in the paths of fame,*
> *Bloody dissectors, worse than ten Monroes;*
> *He hacks to teach, they mangle to expose.*[21]

The three Alexander Monroes – father, son and grandson – *Primus*, *Secondus* and *Tertius* – were professors of anatomy at Edinburgh from 1721 to 1859. Although sound teachers, to Burns they represent the underlying fear of people with medical skill, real or assumed: the Monroes carve human flesh and physicians prescribe poisons.

Quackery was different from the physic of the physician, however: it involved theatre and the sudden, dramatic intervention in the course of an illness or an increasing infirmity.[22] Quack doctors had been active all over Europe for hundreds of years, travelling from town to town, proclaiming their unique powers, allowing an assistant to pretend that he had been saved by the principal actor, and then selling remedies or offering physical manipulations that were certain to alter the life of the sufferer. They amazed, they made their promises, and left a cloud of wonder and hope, usually followed by lingering disappointment. It is right to be cynical about their extravagant claims, and the quacks were certainly cynical about the people whose money they took. Their basic skill was not in medicine, but in attracting attention: many quacks had been acrobats.

This form of quack medicine was a kind of street theatre. The performers sprang and jumped in crazy costumes, to make people think about lively movement and the state of the human body. Once a crowd had gathered, the mountebanks held sway with what Ebenezer Picken of Paisley called the 'gibbi-gabble rhetoricism'[23] of exaggerated language and surprising claims as to what their wares could do. Another man used verbal acrobatics to sell his nostrums, as Picken put it:

> *Whene'er the carle told his tale,* [man]
> *He gar a silence aye prevail;*
> *An' bodies drank his skilled oration,*
> *Like stories tauld be inspiration.*[24]

In 1785 a salesman appeared in Ayrshire. Dr McGill, a 'stage doctor' from Doune in Perthshire (with the possible implication that he had access to ancient Highland wisdom), presented himself both as a fool and a wise man, selling pills that would cure anything.[25] One wonders if he had assumed the name of the minister of Ayr, William McGill, as a way of suggesting learning and status.

A minority of quacks, however, did have real skills to offer their patients. At the highest level, quack doctors were public figures, and some of the most celebrated English characters reached Edinburgh.[26] They included Edward Green the oculist (who also cured stammerers) in 1728, and 'the Chevalier' Taylor [see *fig.* 12] in 1744 who treated the poor free of charge in a public space – the Magdalen Chapel in the Cowgate – chosen because it enabled an audience to have a clear view of him demonstrating his skill. The most successful were often eye surgeons. This speciality, however, was no promise of success, and when Burns was on his Border tour he met a man at Jedburgh who had been blinded by a travelling oculist.[27] Travelling dentists also worked by the same methods, although in their case the offer of sudden release from pain by tooth pulling was justified.

One of the most famous quacks was a Scot, James Graham, born in the Cowgate in Edinburgh, who made and discarded fortunes in London, was an enthusiast for cure by electricity, and later for the use of mud baths using the old idea that contact made under the earth gave strength to the human frame. He came back to his native city in 1784/85, and died there in 1794.

In the eighteenth century the older form of quackery was replaced by the selling of patent medicines, often made in London, as a well-organised commercial operation. Many were strong versions of medicine in the dispensatory; and chemicals like antimony, mercury and opium were their active ingredients, often in dangerously large quantities. James's Powder, which contained garlic, balsam and sarsaparilla, was said to have made King George III mad. Lowther's nervous powder included powdered bone ground from human skulls (possibly the commercial exploitation of a supernatural idea, for witches took human fat and marrow for their preparations). One of the most profitable ventures was the Cordial Balm of Gilead, actually brandy and herbs. This was made in Liverpool by Samuel Solomon, who advertised it in his *Guide to Health* (*c.*1796) and in newspapers all over the country, including the Dumfries *Weekly Journal*.[28]

The quack was easily parodied, although scepticism about his power was usually found in the city rather than in the less critical countryside:

> *It was I, that cured Prester John's juggler's wife's waiting woman of a fistula in her elbow of which she dy'd. ... It was I, that cured the Morocco embassador of a lapsa lingua. It was me, and only me, that cured the French dancing-man, at Amsterdam, of a corruption* [i.e. a hole] *in his pocket.*[29]

This is mocking an audience that is only too willing to believe the patter. They are ignorant, for the Moroccan ambassador had no greater lapse than a slip of the tongue, and the dancer's problem was probably solved by the loan of a few coppers.

One of the best-informed attacks on quackery was made by a man who may have known Burns, Dr James Makittrick Adair (1728-1801). Burns certainly knew his son (1765-1802), who had the same name. Adair the elder made his career as a fashionable physician in England, particularly at Bath. He believed that patent medicines did harm, and he also defended his profession from the free-for-all world in which anyone could set themselves up as a medical practitioner.

By 1786, when Burns wrote 'Death and Dr Hornbook', untrained imitators who pretended they were learned doctors but behaved like quacks were appearing in the countryside. The poem is an explicit attack on a man who had no medical training but still practised medicine. It also implicitly praises John Mackenzie, the man who had attended his father, for his knowledge, humanity and honesty, all of which Hornbook lacks. A Dumfriesshire minister was aware of the same problem when he complained that 'the want of a thorough bred skilful practitioner' in his country parish left the way open for 'illiterate pretenders to medical science'.[30]

John Hornbook is a mixture of several forms of incompetence. Death complained of Hornbook that: 'He's grown sae weel acquaint wi' Buchan / An' ither chaps.'[31] He is an untrained version of the well-meaning father or mother at the head of a family, for whom William Buchan had written his *Domestic Medicine* (1769). Buchan was an Edinburgh-trained physician who wanted people to look after themselves with sensible diet and exercise, and if needs be to treat their family and servants when they were ill. Buchan saw this as a supplement to professional attention. Hornbook, by implication, did not.

Hornbook's cures were those of a trained surgeon and physician – surgical instruments and strange drugs with impressive names. Death described them:

> And then a' doctor's saws an' whittles,
> Of a' dimensions, shapes, an' mettles,
> A' kind o' boxes, mugs, an' bottles,
>   He's sure to hae;
> Their Latin names as fast he rattles
>   As A B C.[32]

This already sounds dangerous. Death himself has a 'whittle', and it may be that Hornbook in his ineptitude can cut the thread of life too. There is a comic plenitude in him having one of every kind of implement and drug. This makes him sound even more like a tradesman: the collection of saws, planes and knives in the workshop of a carpenter or wheelwright was baffling to the layman.

But as well as the regular apparatus of professional medicine, this

'Doctor' has a lot of useless things which he names, starting with ...

> *Calces o' fossils, earths, and trees;*
> *True sal-marinum o' the seas;*
> *The farina of beans and pease,*
>   *He has't in plenty;*
> *Aqua-fontis, what you please,*
>   *He can content ye.*[33]

'Salmarinum' is salt, 'aqua-fontis' is water from a fountain (not 'aqua-fortis', although perhaps that is what Hornbook intended to have, for 'aqua-fortis' is sulphuric acid). A 'calx' is a substance which has been thoroughly burned to drive off all its volatile parts, and a 'farina' is no more than a powder. Hornbook has book learning, and he has the apparatus of knives and medicines, but he does not have understanding.

One quack was lampooned for selling the 'purandos tankapon tolos', the 'excellent quality of which, is hardly known, even to myself'. It was 'good against all sanguine, melancholy, phlematic, or choleric humour'; but more than that, this remarkable drug was 'sudorific, cathartic, specific, amaradulphic, absetergic, mundific, and apperiatic'.[34] These words were intended to suggest a high level of education, a sophisticated understanding of the powers of the diverse components of the preparation, and a profound awareness of the many balances which the physician had all at once to maintain, like an acrobat manipulating plates spinning on the end of bamboo sticks. This is the stage on which Hornbook walked, where a showy pattern of Greek and Latin adjectives suggested mystery.

Death goes on to say:

> *Where I kill'd ane, a fair strae-death,*   [natural death in bed]
> *By loss o' blood or want o' breath,*
> *This night I'm free to tak my aith,*
>   *That Hornbook's skill*
> *Has clad a score i' their last claith,*   [last cloth, i.e. shroud]
>   *By drap and pill.*[35]

Death operates naturally and gains nothing for his labour beyond his daily wage. Hornbook is more enterprising, receiving payment by results:

A country laird had ta'en the batts, [colic, i.e. stomach ache]
Or some curmurring in his guts,
His only son for Hornbook sets,
    An' pays him well:
The lad, for twa guid gimmer-pets, [female sheep bet. 1st/2nd shearing]
    Was laird himsel.[36]

So Hornbook is different from the physician, who was committed to the welfare of his patient, although one hopes that it was Hornbook's inept treatment that caused the father's death, rather than a case of deliberate murder.

The word *curmurring* is based on 'murr', the purring of a cat, and 'curr' intensifies it. There are other examples in Scots of using two similar or rhyming words to create emphasis, like *mixter-maxter* or *argle-bargle*. *Curmurring* is also an example of onomatopoeia, like the medical term for the sound of a rumbling stomach, *borborygm*, from the Greek. Hornbook has latched on to the symptom of the rumbling belly without wondering what has caused it.

Hornbook has some characteristics of the Devil, and indeed the second verse can be read as saying that the whole poem is about him:

But this that I am gaun to tell,
Which lately on a night befell,
Is just as true's the Deil's in hell
    Or Dublin city:
That e'er he nearer comes oursel
    'S a muckle pity![37]

Hornbook's name can also be shortened to 'Hornie', like 'Auld Hornie', and his incompetence is like that of the folk Devil.

Folk medicine, on the other hand, was quite different from quackery, and highly diverse. It included the use of herbs picked locally, drinking well water, and various practices we can retrospectively label magic. The distinguishing feature of folk medicine was that knowledge of it was held by the people as a whole. When an individual was particularly well-informed – say an old woman who had a lifetime's worth of experience – she held the knowledge on behalf of the community. It was not in the hands of a few professionals or entrepreneurs who saw it as a source of cash. However, if the community believed that a woman had, say, wisdom in the use of herbs that she would not share with others, then she was on the way to becoming a witch.

Here is an example of the magical side of folk medicine. The wife of a minister in Nithsdale bore a son who yawned all day, to the point where there was concern about his health. The midwife – someone who knew the lore of childbirth – asked whether the mother had *greened* [longed for] anything to eat while she was pregnant. A sheep's head was the answer. So a head was brought in and boiled, and the meat rubbed over the child's lips, and thus the cure was made. As so often with folk medicine, it is not clear why the action was successful, but it was. However, this was true of formal medicine too.[38]

Various amulets or charms protected people and animals from witchcraft.[39] Flint arrowheads, thought of as elf-arrows, have already been mentioned [see *fig.* 30]. The advice was given: 'Just sew that within the lining of your stays, lady; or in the band of your petticoat; and there'll be nobody can harm you.' An arrowhead worn by a Galloway farmer, suspended from a collar of horsehair, is in the collections of National Museums Scotland. The health of children was safeguarded by sewing into their clothes a heart of lead or silver. Anything unusual could be interpreted as having a supernatural origin and so bearing supernatural powers. Strangely-shaped stones and unfamiliar nuts and seeds washed ashore by the Gulf Stream, were other examples. Charms could also be used aggressively, like the calf's heart from near Edinburgh, given to National Museums Scotland in 1827. Dozens of pins are stuck in it, perhaps for malign purposes [see *fig.* 29].

Burns owned an amulet, a 'Stone of bluish colour, covered with a Christal, & set in Silver – upon the Stone is a figure representing the letter 'Z' [see *fig.* 31]. One of the most famous is the Lee Penny, an English silver coin of *c.*1300 with a dark red stone mounted in it. The stone is said to have been brought from Spain by Sir Symon Loccard [Lockhart] who carried the key to the casket containing the heart of Robert Bruce when it was taken into battle against the Moors in 1329. The issue of the use of the stone as possibly being superstitious was brought before the General Assembly of the Kirk at Glasgow in 1638. When it was dipped in water, it was done 'without using onie wordes such as charmers and sourcerers use in their Unlawful Practicess'. This decided the matter. The ministers reasoned that 'in nature they are many thinges sain to work strange effect qr of no human wit can give a reason, it having pleased God to give unto stones & herbes a special Vertue for the healings of mony Infirmities in man and beast', so it was considered safe to continue to use the Lee Penny.[40]

Some stones, such as ones with a magical origin, could cure illness. A Galloway laird, whose land was near Balmaclellan, took the eggs from a crow's nest, boiled them hard and returned them. The crow deserted the dead eggs, but in a while returned and left a stone in the nest: by implication it had come from a distance and was therefore exotic. The stone was thereafter used to ease the pains of women in childbirth. However, when it was tried on a whelping bitch, it cracked and fell to pieces.[41] The magic stone had been insulted.

There was one small book which bridged a form of learned medicine and folk medicine: *Tippermalluch's Receipts* by John Moncrieff of Tippermalluch, first printed in 1715. The book contained a miscellany of advice from various sources, some taken from a volume written to a priest who reigned briefly as Pope John XXI from 1276 to 1277. Tippermalluch included exotic herbs and other ingredients that would not have been available in a typical Scottish town: in other words, his book shows what is possible rather than what can be realised. It is also flavoured with magic, recommending, for example, that St John's wort be hung in the house to put evil spirits to flight. Carrying 'eringo' [sea holly] protects against witchcraft, and 'those enchanted since birth' will be helped by carrying a magnet. Tippermalluch has one quality in common with the quack: he boasts of 'stupendous cures'.

In the Middle Ages the Church had recognised the healing powers of wells or springs of fresh water. Most well water was especially effective on the quarter days, and on Beltane (1 May) most of all. Some wells were named after local saints, and the ones with the best reputation became the destinations for pilgrimages. These wells kept their pre-Reformation names: there were two Lady's wells near Kirkoswald, and south-west of Dumfries St Querdon's retains its name to this day. When the latter was cleared out in Victorian times, coins were found from the reign of Elizabeth of England onwards, including ones from the reign of George III. It had been visited 300 years earlier, and was still part of the medicine of Burns's time.

A few wells were known all over the country and people came to them on pilgrimage from great distances. King Robert Bruce travelled to Kingscase near Prestwick, where he received benefit from the well water, and there were still a few huts there for drinkers late in the eighteenth century.[42] These wells were powerful places, portals to the other world; a source of pure water, seen as a gift from deep in the earth.

By the eighteenth century Scottish physicians had come to believe in the benefits of visiting spas to drink mineral water. Some old healing wells took on this new role, in which the drinking of water was a central part of the cure, along with a controlled diet and exercise such as walking or horse-riding. Some wells provided water flavoured by minerals: their water was unusual and so might be supposed to have special powers. Many wells were said to be good for skin complaints such as scrofula.[43] In his dying days, Burns went to Brow Well, nine miles from Dumfries. It was only a few yards from the sea and he could bathe there too.

Folk medicine was all but killed by professional practice. Sick people needed to have their illnesses understood and if possible cured, and the physician could do it more effectively than anyone else. The respect previously shown to the wise woman was transferred to the general practitioner, who was to become a figure of authority in the country community, in time more powerful than the minister.

NOTES

1 *Old Statistical Account*: Kilmarnock.
2 OSA: Ballantrae.
3 OSA: Sorn.
4 *Dumfries Weekly Journal (DWJ)*, 20 January 1789, 3a.
5 Wodrow (1842-43), vol. 4, p. 301.
6 Ibid.
7 OSA: Ayr.
8 OSA: Cummertrees, Glencairn.
9 OSA: Dunscore.
10 Burnett (2007-08).
11 Robertson (1904), p. 86; Kinsley (1968), p. 54.
12 DWJ, 10 June 1789, 1a.
13 Ibid., 12 June 1778, 4a.
14 OSA: Morton.
15 OSA: Ballantrae.
16 Fenton (2007), pp. 372-85.
17 Wodrow (1842-43), vol. 4, p. 203.
18 OSA: Mauchline.
19 Fergusson (1807), p. 286.
20 Robertson (1904), p. 207; Kinsley (1968), p. 586.
21 Ibid. (1904), p. 207; (1968), p. 587.
22 Porter (2000).
23 Picken (1788), p. 173.
24 Ibid.
25 Steven (1899), p. 45.
26 Thin (1938).
27 Mackay (1992), p. 309.
28 DWJ, 3 July 1798, 4c.
29 *The Harangues* .... (1762), p. 10.
30 OSA: Kirkconnel.
31 Robertson (1904), p. 64; Kinsley (1968), p. 81.
32 Ibid. (1904), p. 65; (1968), p. 82.
33 Ibid. (1904); (1968).
34 *The Harangues* .... (1762), p. 9.
35 Robertson (1904), p. 66; Kinsley (1968), p. 83.
36 Ibid. (1904); (1968).
37 Ibid. (1904), p. 62; (1968), p. 79.
38 Wodrow (1842-43), vol. 4, p. 93.
39 Black (1892-93).
40 Reid (1922-23).
41 Wodrow (1842-43), vol. 2, 87.
42 Loch (1778), p. 89.
43 e.g. OSA: Langholm.

CHAPTER 7

The Year

*To everything there is a season, and a
time to every purpose under heaven.*

THE country community was intensely aware of the seasons, because
they defined the year's work. Physical comfort, with limited sources
of light and heat, was also affected by them. Holidays, too, were part of
the structure of the year, days when people stepped out of their daily
role and did something different. There was

A time to weep, and a time to laugh;
a time to mourn and a time to dance.

References to the time of year and characteristic weather are
frequent in Burns's poems and songs. On 1 April 1785 he wrote to John
Lapraik of 'briers an' woodbines budding green'. 'The Twa Dogs' is
set on 'A bonie day in June', 'The Holy Fair' 'upon a simmer Sunday
morn', and 'The Jolly Beggars' begins:

When lyart leaves bestrow the yird, [multicoloured]
Or, wavering like the baukie bird [bat]
Bedim cauld Boreas' blast.[1] [the north wind]

This is one of many of his descriptions of early winter. Another is in 'The Brigs of Ayr':

> 'Twas when the stacks get on their winter-hap,
> And thack and rape secure the toil-won crap; [rope, crop]
> Potatoe-bings are snugged up frae skaith [harm]
> O' coming Winter's biting, frosty breath.[2]

The cycle of the seasons controlled work and where it was done. From the Middle Ages until not long before Burns was born, the number of animals had been sharply reduced at the beginning of winter, partly by the sale of beasts for the English market, but also by the killing of many of the others for salting. The ballad 'Get up and Bar the Door' starts with a reference to the feast of St Martin on 11 November:

> It fell about the Martinmas time,
> And a gay time it was then,
> When our goodwife got puddings to make,
> And she's boiled them in the pan.[3]

The 'puddings' are meaty sausages, made from the animals that have just been killed.

Until the cultivation of the turnip became widespread, there was not enough feed to keep all the animals alive until the spring grass began to grow. Except around midwinter, the land was ploughed. The draught oxen, and the horses that replaced them, were given much of the small quantity of available food so that they were strong enough to draw the plough. Apart from this, a minimum of work was done outside: in those harsh winters there were many kinds and quantities of snow and ice and they inhibited labour in various ways. Restricted to indoors, the farmer mended and made, and waited for the chance to be in the open air again.

Spring was a blessed release and a period of high activity. The ploughing continued. It was in April 1786, for example, that Burns turned over the flower which he addressed in 'To a Mountain Daisy'. The corn was sown; the turnips and potatoes planted. After a few weeks the turnips were *shawed*, the slow process of cutting off the leaves so that all the plants' energy went into the tuber. Animals were released into the fields and gave birth. It was the season of lamb and calf, fledgling and shoot.

Plants grew and animals grazed in summer. The work on the farm was not so directly tied to the production of food as in spring or autumn. At the beginning of the eighteenth century it had been a slack time of year, when the women still had the regular tasks of butter- and cheese-making, but men might not be so busy. By the 1780s, however, the summer months were the opportunity for improving the farm in a dozen ways, like ploughing land which had not been ploughed before, or digging ditches to drain the land.

Autumn was the time to reap, when the corn was sheared, stooked and stacked. The earth had produced, and the corn had to be brought in. But the harvest weather was sometimes poor:

> While at the stook the shearers cow'r
> To shun the bitter blaudin' show'r.[4] [beating]

A fine summer with sufficient rain might be negated by bad weather in the harvest month. It was also an emotional time of year, when people could assess the food supply for the coming winter, and the profit for the farm.

To name a season was to indicate the work being done and the state of mind of the people. 'The Ballad of Otterburne' begins:

> It fell about the Lammas tide
> When the muir men win their hay.[5]

This tells us that the events took place at the beginning of August, but it says more than that. The farmers on the lower ground have already harvested their hay. The 'muir men' are free for an expedition, but not for a long campaign: in a month their corn will be ripe, and the most anxious weeks will have arrived, with the intense work of bringing in that year's crop. The community could not survive without the food, so the men who have gone off to steal cattle in England will be back in their own fields soon.

Early winter was a significant time for Burns.

> When chill November's surly blast
> Made fields and forests bare.[6]

The natural world was closing up and shutting down for the nights of

17

18

17. Robert Burns

Miniature portrait by Alexander Reid, c.1795-96, detail. Watercolour on ivory.

The Burns family moved from Ellisland Farm to Dumfries in November 1791, so that the poet might concentrate on his Excise work. This moving portrait, painted in the last months of Burns's life, shows the effects of the fatal rheumatic heart disease from which he was suffering.

(SCOTTISH NATIONAL PORTRAIT GALLERY)

18. 'The Grave of Robert Fergusson' (1750-74)

Steel engraving from a painting by J. Drummond RSA, c.1850.

Burns's response to the untimely death of Fergusson in an Edinburgh asylum, was to pay for a headstone at the unmarked grave in Canongate churchyard in 1789.

(DUMFRIES MUSEUM)

19. Earthenware bowl

Clyde Pottery, Greenock, Renfrewshire. Second half of the 19th century.

Decorated with scenes and lines from 'Tam o' Shanter', such products were part of a thriving Burns 'industry' which continues to this day.

(NATIONAL MUSEUMS SCOTLAND)

19

20. The Mauchline holy fair

Oil painting by Alexander Carse, *c.*1830.

Depicting scenes from Burns's poem 'The Holy Fair'; the event took place in August and lasted several days. Large numbers came from local parishes, attending preaching and prayer meetings prior to taking communion.

(NATIONAL TRUST FOR SCOTLAND)

Detail a.

People in their best clothes arriving at the holy fair.

Detail b.

Minister preaching at the holy fair:

> '*Hear how he clears the points o' faith*
> *Wi' rattlin' and wi' thumpin'!*'

(Robert Burns)

21. Alexander Carse

Group portrait on panel.

Probably Alexander Carse with his mother and sister, *c.*1795.

This intimate and moving scene shows the two women protectively enclosing the artist, all of whom in turn are surrounded by objects relating to the gifted son's career. The senior family member reads from The Holy Bible, recalling scenes from 'The Cotter's Saturday Night'.

Carse shared Burns's interest in the life and traditions of rural Scotland.

(SCOTTISH NATIONAL PORTRAIT GALLERY)

22. Masonic jug (said to have belonged to Robert Burns)

White earthenware.

The poet became a mason in 1781 and remained involved throughout his life. Many of his most influential connections were made through freemasonry.

(DUMFRIES MUSEUM)

23. Woodblock by Thomas Bewick

Used for the first Liverpool edition of *The Works of Robert Burns*, edited by James Currie, 1800.

Bewick's combination of plough and sickle, together with a masonic emblem of bees and beehive, makes a deft juxtaposition of significant elements in Burns's life.

(NATIONAL TRUST FOR SCOTLAND)

24. New map of Ayrshire, 1775

By Andrew Armstrong.

Tam o' Shanter's route from Ayr to Alloway on Armstrong's map.

The road to Kirk Alloway and the bridge over the Doon runs south from Ayr past Fairfield (roughly where Thomas Kennedy of Colzean was murdered), and it fords the Slaphouse Burn ('Whare in the snaw the chapman smoor'd').

The 'ruin' near the bottom of the map is Kirk Alloway.

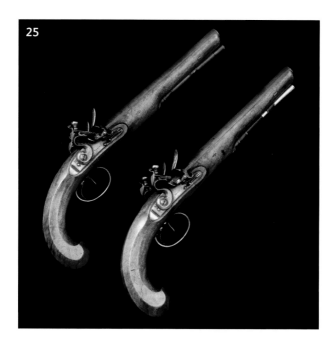

25. Pistols owned by Robert Burns

Pair of double-barrelled pistols owned by Burns, when he was an exciseman, 1789-96.

Made by David Blair, 1788, and given to the poet. The Birmingham gunsmith, like Burns, was a staunch radical. 'The defensive tools do more than half of mankind do, they do honour to their maker.' (Burns)

(NATIONAL MUSEUMS SCOTLAND)

26. 'The Deil's awa wi the Exciseman'

Watercolour by Thomas Stothard, c.1814.

Burns could see the irony in his own situation as an employee of the State.

It is easy to imagine how cleverly this colourful Devil, in his jester's clothes, and accompanied by his retinue of musical imps, could play reels, horn-pipes and strathspeys, and lead us all on a merry dance.

(NATIONAL GALLERY OF SCOTLAND)

27. Blacksmith's headstone, Alloway

The tools of the smith's trade are realistically
depicted on this stone: including anvil, hammer
and pincers.

(NATIONAL MUSEUMS SCOTLAND)

28. Agate buttons owned by Robert Burns

With markings often resembling an eye, agates were worn to protect against the 'evil eye'. It was also believed that agates made their wearers agreeable and persuasive.

(NATIONAL TRUST FOR SCOTLAND)

29. Calf's heart stuck with pins

From Dalkeith, Midlothian. A remnant of supernatural belief from the 19th century.

(NATIONAL MUSEUMS SCOTLAND)

30. Flint arrowhead

Often prized as 'elf arrow' amulets for their supposed magical properties, these were in reality Neolithic flints, unearthed during ploughing.

Water in which they were dipped was also considered beneficial.

(NATIONAL MUSEUMS SCOTLAND)

31. Amulet belonging to Robert Burns

Drawing by Adam de Cardonnel, pencil and watercolour, 1820.

One of the founder members of the Society of Antiquaries of Scotland, and a friend of Burns, Cardonnel was also a travelling companion of fellow antiquarian, Francis Grose.

The amulet is described as a 'magical gem' belonging to 'the Airshire bard'. Perhaps it was worn for luck, or the symbols may have had masonic significance.

(NATIONAL MUSEUMS SCOTLAND)

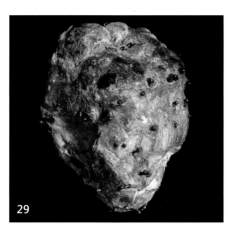

29

30

31

32. The Brig o' Doon and Burns Monument

Oil painting by David Roberts, 1862 [detail].

A herd of Ayrshire cattle follow Tam o' Shanter's route over the River Doon. The ruined gables of Kirk Alloway are shown on the skyline to the left of the Brig.

The Burns Monument, designed by Thomas Hamilton, was opened in 1823. The cost of over £3350 was met by public subscription.

long northern darkness when frosts nip, clothes dry slowly and rheumatism seeps into the bones. Burns imagined a storm:

While, tumbling brown, the burn comes down,
And roars frae bank to brae:
And bird and beast in covert rest,
And pass the heartless day.[7]

Here he is using one of his most effective techniques, allowing the state of nature to represent his own emotional condition. He also wrote of early winter as the time when the human race destroyed parts of the natural world. The friendly bees, having made their honey,

Are doom'd by Man, that tyrant o'er the weak,
The death o' devils, smoor'd wi' brimstone reek:
The thund'ring guns are heard on ev'ry side,
The wounded coveys, reeling, scatter wide.[8]

Burns was also explicit about his feelings. 'About the "gloomy month of November, when the people of England [i.e. Britain] hang and drown themselves," any thing generally is better than one's own thoughts'.[9] One winter, probably 1793, he wrote to Maria Riddell: 'I sit, altogether Novemberish, a dam'd melange of Fretfulness & melancholy; not enough of the one to arouse me to passion, nor of the other to repose me in torpor; my soul flouncing & fluttering round her tenement, like a wild finch caught amid the horrors of winter & newly thrust into a cage'.[10] October had been a bleak month for Burns: his youngest brother John died in October 1785, 'Highland Mary' in 1786, and Robert's first daughter Jean in 1787.

In the Middle Ages the Catholic Church had built up a sophisticated calendar that controlled the liturgy.[11] It was based on three elements: the Christmas cycle which focused on the birth of Jesus Christ on 25 December; the Easter cycle which started on Shrove Tuesday, centred on Easter Sunday, and ended seven weeks later with Whitsunday; and the feast days of the saints throughout the year. In cathedrals, and in abbey churches like the one at Crossraguel near Kirkoswald, and collegiate churches such as Lincluden between Dumfries and Ellisland, the major holidays had been celebrated with pomp and spectacle, and often with lavish meals for the participants.

In Scotland this came to an end with the Protestant Reformation. Anything which hinted at ritual was suppressed, so all the prominent parts of the Catholic calendar were removed, including Christmas and Easter, although some old holidays did survive in modified form. From 1560 onwards, however, secular events were more conspicuous, particularly fairs. The purpose of a fair was to enable the buying and selling of livestock and goods: farm people brought things like the cloth and grass rope which they had made during the winter, and took away kitchen utensils and other objects which were made by specialist tradesmen. Whereas saints had their feasts on fixed days like St Michael on 29 September, fairs were usually defined by formulae like 'the second Tuesday in June', so that they could never fall on a Sunday.

The abolition of Christmas at the Reformation meant that the hitherto lesser holiday of the New Year became the most important midwinter holiday in Scotland. There were no communal events like the great religious services at Christmas, but instead a day of rest when neighbours and families ate together. Burns's contemporary, Ebeneezer Picken, said that at that time country people might hope to have nappy ale, currant buns, and three-year-old kebbucks [cheeses], rich and full of mites.[12] Christmas had been a celebration of birth, but the New Year was more of a recognition of the passage of time, as in Burns's 'The Auld Farmer's New-Year Morning Salutation to his Auld Mare, Maggie':

> Tho' now thou's dowie, stiff, an' crazy, [slow]
> An' thy auld hide's as white's a daisie,
> I've seen thee dappled, sleek an' glaizie, [glossy]
>   A bonnie grey.[13]

As this poem shows, it was also the opportunity to affirm the bond with animals as well as with humans.

In 1752 a new calendar was introduced, adjusting the old one by 11 days. As a result, holidays were celebrated by some people at their 'old' date and by others at the new one. In north-east Scotland, the one Lowland area where Christmas continued to be celebrated, 'Aul Eel' [old Yule] survived well into the nineteenth century, and in Argyllshire 'Old New Year's Day' was still alive round the First World War.

After the Catholic calendar had been abandoned, fragments of the older, pagan Celtic calendar remained in the form of the four quarter days. They were not holidays, but they were known to all and were part of the framework of the year. Candlemas (2 February) survived in schools in the eighteenth century. It had been the feast when the church was filled with candles, 'the Candlemass bleeze', but it became the day on which each boy paid the schoolmaster for the winter's heating and lighting of the schoolroom. Beltane (1 May) was the second most important Celtic day. After the Reformation bonfires continued to be lit on Beltane, and it was the day for visiting healing wells, when their water was supposed to be at its most powerful. The third of the quarter days, Lammas, is on 1 August. Lammas meant both the day and the period around it: the latter is what Burns meant when he wrote:

> *It was upon a Lammas night*
> *When corn rigs are bonnie.*[14]

... that is, the corn has grown well and promises a good harvest. Samhuin (1 November) had been the beginning of the Celtic year, and when All Hallows ceased to be celebrated the supernatural importance of the old holiday was remembered. The Celtic day had started at nightfall, like the day in the Bible, so people held festivities on Halloween – the evening before All Hallows.

For administrative purposes All Hallows was replaced as a quarter day by Martinmas, and it was on Martinmas 1791 that Burns moved to Dumfries. Similarly, Beltane was linked to one of the key days in the administrative calendar, confusingly known as Whitsunday despite the fact that in eighteenth-century Scotland it was held on a fixed date: 15 May from 1693 to 1752, and 29 May after that. Whitsunday was 'term day' in south-west Scotland, when farmers and farm servants moved. Again, it was Whitsunday 1788 when Burns took possession of Ellisland.

Fastern's E'en, the Scottish Shrove Tuesday, had been in the Middle Ages the day before the beginning of the self-denial of Lent. After the Reformation it was no more than a minor marker of the passage from winter into spring. It usually fell in February. Like some other Scottish holidays, it did not involve stopping work, but instead a sociable meeting of neighbours in the evening, during which work continued. This is what Burns described in the 'Epistle to J. Lapraik':

> *On* Fastens een *we had a rockin,* [gathering to spin wool]
> *To ca' the crack and weave our stockin;*
> *And there was muckle fun and jokin,*

> *Ye need na doubt;*
> *At length we had a hearty yoking,* [leisure period]
> *At 'sang about'.*[15]

Fastern's E'en was enjoyed indoors, a winter pleasure like the winter work being done beside the fire.

There were also local holidays, and they had all kinds of roots. The horse race at Kirkpatrick Fleming stemmed from the feast of the saint, Patrick, to whom the medieval church had been dedicated. At Irvine, Marymass was originally the Feast of the Assumption of the Virgin (the day on which she was received into heaven): somehow these two holidays, and most surprisingly the use of their names, had been allowed to continue despite the assumption of the Protestant religion. Another example is Colmsday at Largs, named after St Colm-Cille, otherwise Columba. Like Marymass it was one parish's holiday, but it drew people from a distance:

> *Great numbers of people, from 40 or 50 miles round, resort to it,*
> *some for business, some for pleasure. Upwards of 100 boats are*
> *often to be seen, on this occasion, riding in the bay.*[16]

The boats had brought people and livestock from Arran, Kintyre and Cowal. At Ayr one of the chief events of the year was Midsummer fair. It too brought people from Arran and Kintyre, and similarly it was held at the time of year when the long days made travel easier. The Groset fair at Kilmarnock was held at the time when gooseberries were ripe, and so were for sale at the Fair. In the 1740s the carters of Newton-on-Ayr found that they had a good trade in carrying kippered salmon inland, and at the end of the salmon-fishing season they treated themselves to the delicacy they had been selling. Calling the day 'Kipper fair', they raced their horses on the sands and held a dance in the evening. At this event, the whisky circulated in a pail.

There were two kinds of holiday that were not fixed in the calendar. One was the curling match, when the earth was frozen hard and could not be ploughed or harrowed. When the millpond was a sheet of ice and a likely venue for the play, men went out at sunrise, staying until

> *The sun had closed the winter day,*
> *The curlers quat their roarin' play.*[17]

The other such holiday was Holy Communion, held in summer on a different day in each parish. The Catholic Church held communion every week, but the reformers made it special by holding it once a year. There was also a practical reason for Communion being infrequent, for each one depended on having several ministers present, to preach and to dispense the sacrament.

Up to the time of Burns's childhood, ministers went round their parish to hold a 'diet of examine' in the weeks before communion. A group of people sat in a house in the evening and the minister asked them questions about religious doctrine and the Bible. It was a test of knowledge, faith and orthodoxy. It helped people to understand the solemnity of communion, and enabled the minister to detect who among his flock were not prepared for it. The diet was a solemn occasion, but when the minister left, the fiddle was tuned and songs followed.[18]

Communion drew people from neighbouring parishes and the numbers could be large. At the Mauchline holy fair Burns described in 1786, perhaps one-third were from other parishes. The number of communicants was 1400, and if the adults who did not take communion are added, and the children who were too young to do so, the total present was probably nearer 4000.[19] Even the Mauchline horse race did not draw so many. The resulting experience was an assault on the senses and emotions. Each person was

> ... forced to wrestle through a crowd, to push and be pushed, stunned with a general hubbub, the seats rattling, the galleries sounding, the people singing, the communicants jostling one another in the crowded passages, some falling, fainting and in all corners of the church, hurry, confusion, and noise.[20]

In 'The Holy Fair', Burns describes the mixture of the spiritual and secular [see *fig.* 20]:

> *Here some are thinkin' on their sins,*
> *An' some upo' their claes;*
> *Ane curses feet that fyl'd his shins,* [fouled]
> *Anither sighs an' prays:*
> *On this hand sits a chosen swatch,*
> *Wi screw'd up, grace-proud faces;*
> *On that a set o' chaps, at watch,*

> *Thrang winkin' on the lasses*
>   *To chairs that day.*[21]

One of the preachers is the Auld Licht John Russell, otherwise 'Black Jock':

> *His talk o' Hell, where devils dwell,*
> *Our very 'sauls does harrow'*
>   *Wi' fright that day!*[22]

Burns is referring to the appearance of the ghost of Hamlet's father, who tells his son that he cannot reveal the nature of Hell:

> *I could a tale unfold whose lightest word*
> *Would harrow up thy soul, freeze thy young blood,*
> *Make thy two eyes, like stars, start from their spheres.*[23]

The ghost of a king may not be able to reveal Hell, but Jock Russell can: he recreates in Mauchline the experience of being there:

> *A vast, unbottom'd, boundless pit,*
> *Fill'd fou o' lowin' brunstane,*
> *Wha's ragin' flame, an' scorchin' heat,*
> *Wad melt the hardest whun-stane!*
> *The half-asleep start up wi' fear,*
> *An' think they hear it roarin',*
> *When presently it does appear*
> *'Twas but some neebor snorin'*
>   *Asleep that day.*[24]

At the end of 'The Holy Fair', Burns says that the gathering has also enabled young people to encounter one another, with the likelihood that couples will meet in the future:

> *An' mony jobs that day begin,*
> *May end in houghmagandie*
>   *Some ither day.*[25]

Another commentator did not believe sexual satisfaction was delayed:

What must the consequence be, when a whole country side is thrown loose, and young fellows and girls are going home together by night, the gayest season of the year; when every thing naturally inspires warm designs and silence, secrecy and darkness encourage them?[26]

Communion tokens were a minor art form, like small coins [see *fig.* 10].[27] The elders gave them to adults who were judged to be in a fit spiritual state to receive holy communion, and on communion Sunday they were admission tickets. Usually made of lead, they were struck locally with a crude punch or cast in a mould, and each parish had its own design, usually bearing no more than its name. However, some, particularly in south-west Scotland, had symbols on their tokens. The Ayr token (1747) had on one side a communion cup with 'John 6.35' – 'I am the bread of life', and on the other a loaf of bread and another verbal reference to communion bread standing for the body of Christ.[28] Carsphairn had a communion cup and loaf, and a reference to Psalm 9.11 ('Sing praises to the Lord, which dwelleth in Zion'). Kilwinning's token showed a bunch of grapes. Most tokens were square or rectangular, but some Galloway parishes had heart-shaped ones. Anwoth's had a bleeding heart (1755) with the initials of Robert Carson, minister and smuggler.

How can we understand the role of the communion token? It was not worn, like a badge, yet the parish knew who had not been given tokens; and it was obvious who had been admitted to take communion on the day, so they gave a public status. Although people who moved from one parish to another were expected to present the minister of the new one with a certificate of character, it has been suggested that communion tokens fulfilled the same function, particularly when someone moved for a short period. However, the most important use of the word 'token' in the Bible was at the end of the Flood, when the rainbow was the token of God's covenant with Noah: the communion token was not a mere token, but a symbol of the path to salvation.

Holidays and special events like holy fairs were considered important, and people looked forward to them. 'The Siller Gun' is a poem by John Mayne, about a shooting competition at Dumfries in 1777 for the trophy of a miniature silver gun. The people anticipated it for months, preparing their clothes for the day.

And turning coats, and mending breeks
New-seating where the sark-tail keeks

> *(Nae matter though the clout that eeks*
> *Be black or blue;)*
> *And darning, with a thousand steeks*
> *The hose anew!* [29]

Even though their clothes are worn, the emotional importance of the holiday is great and they want to look their best. The excitement of the holy fair, too, tells us that it was important to the people who attended it.

In our approach towards 'Tam o' Shanter', we can now turn to the traditional festival, Halloween, on which the poem is based. First, however, we need to remember that some Ayrshire festivals were celebrated with a bonfire. At Tarbolton, a fire was lit on or beside the medieval motte and bailey castle, just north of the village, the evening before the June fair. The school was given a half day to collect firewood, and while the fire burned, groups, particularly of young people, talked and sang. [30] The fire had a practical function: it was a beacon for drovers who were bringing animals to the fair. It was believed to be ancient, and it was said that the name of the parish was derived from *Tor-Beal-Tane*, 'hill of Baal's fire', Baal being an ancient pagan god. In fact, the name is much more likely to be from 'Tor-Bolton' – the hill near the village with buildings. There were fires on the hills round Galston on the evening before December fair. At Dalry they were lit on St Margaret's Day, the last day of July. At Dundonald people made merry round a bonfire on the eve of the Wednesday of Marymass fair at Irvine, and it was still being lit half a century after Burns's death. [31] Finally, bonfires, Halloween *bleezes*, were lit all over the Lowlands to keep away the witches, and to provide amusement. In the dark early winter, the fires could be seen for miles. At Paisley they were on little islands in the River Cart, making sparkling reflections in the water.

Halloween was allowed to continue as the remnant of a Celtic quarter day, with its meaning as the evening before All Hallows' Day discarded. In the pre-Reformation calendar this had been an important period, for All Hallows (or All Saints) was followed by All Souls' day on 2 November. In one place in Galloway, Balmaghie, children begged for food at Halloween: this seems to be a custom adopted from England, where it was called 'souling'. Significant things happened on this day: like the well at Castledykes, Dumfries, which every year dried on Halloween [32]; and events could also be *made* to happen, like the first meeting of the Batchelor's Club that Burns set up in Tarbolton, which was held on Old Halloween in 1780.

People must have been intensely aware of change and continuity during the period around Halloween. It was a more significant time than midwinter, when nothing much was changing and the immediate prospect was of snow and a slight lengthening of the day. Winter was a terrible threat to the community, especially if the harvest had been bad. It was the time of year when people moved from the outdoor world of action to the indoor one of contemplation.

Burns wrote two poems about Halloween – 'Tam o' Shanter' and 'Halloween'. Robert Heron, Burns' contemporary, said the latter was 'the delight of those who are best acquainted with its subject',[33] meaning the country people of south-west Scotland, like himself.

Most of 'Halloween' sets out ways of telling the future, and in particular of foretelling which couples will marry and what sort of relationship they will have.

> Then, first an foremost, thro' the kail, [cabbage]
> Their stocks maun a' be sought ance:
> They steek their een, an' grape an' wale [shut, grope, select]
> For muckle anes an' straught anes.[34]

Burns explained this:

> They [the two young people] must go out, hand in hand, with eyes shut, and pull the first they meet with. Its being big or little, straight or crooked, is prophetic of the size and shape of the grand object of all their spells – the husband or wife. If any yird, or earth, stick to the root, that is tocher, or fortune; and the taste of the custock, that is, the heart of the stem, is indicative of the natural temper and disposition.[35]

Again we see the importance of earth: the more earth, the more life, the better life. Here is another example of what people did:

> Burning the nuts is a famous charm. They name the lad and lass to each particular nut, as they lay them in the fire; and accordingly as they burn quietly together, or start from beside one another, the course and issue of the courtship will be.—R.B.[36]

Or in verse:

> *The auld guidwife's well-hoordit nits*
> *Are round an' round divided,*
> *An' mony lads an' lasses' fates*
> *Are there that night decided:*
> *Some kindle, couthie, side by side,*
> *An' burn thegither trimly;*
> *Some start awa, wi' saucy pride,*
> *An' jump out-owre the chimlie* [chimney]
> *Fu' high that night.*[37]

What Burns is describing in the winter of 1785 as a harmless game could have been seen in a different light earlier in the century. In 1705 at Peninghame, Mary McNair had been found guilty of sorcery: she had been winnowing corn in the barn at Halloween hoping to see an image of the man she was going to marry. This was a ritual called 'Three wechts o' naething' – it meant going to the barn, setting the opposite doors open as though to use the through draught for winnowing corn, and then going through the motions of winnowing corn. When it was done for the third time, as Burns put it, 'an apparition will pass through the barn ... having both the figure in question, and the appearance or retinue, marking the employment or station in life'.[38]

Divination was linked to things that had the power to grow, such as ears of corn or nuts. It was also connected with agents of change or places in which change took place, such as the sickle, or the barn or the kiln; or even things which themselves were going to change beneficially, such as the hay stack which would end up as oatmeal. All of these were close to the Earth. The idea was that the natural world, or more specifically the products of the earth, would produce the answers.

Foretelling the nature of marriage was important to the individual, and marriage (or rather the couple's children) was essential to the continuation of the community. To country people this was of central importance. Marriage often took place on little acquaintance, so guidance as to general appearance or trade was helpful in making a decision. For a woman, her husband's occupation was everything: whether her future involved wealth, or it meant living on a farm or in a village; whether she would be expected work in the fields, or whether her husband had to travel and might be away for half of the year. Would her life involve a move to the town or the city, or perhaps even, as Burns planned for himself and 'Highland Mary' (Margaret Campbell), emigration? The shape of a lifetime might be very variable indeed: illness or injury affected a man's ability to earn his wage, and early death was always possible. Perhaps the haphazard nature of the Halloween rituals also suggested that marriage was a lottery; and certainly these rituals were more romantic than the approach of the greedy young man in one of Burns's songs:

> O, gie me the lass that has acres o charms,
> O, gie me the lass wi the weel-stockit farms.[39]

It may be that as the world began to change, thoughts of the future became of greater concern. People began to realise that they had to make choices, most of which had to be made around the end of adolescence and the time of marriage.

'Tam o' Shanter' is set on Halloween. On Beltane and Halloween, witches met the Devil. By 1 May the nights are short, but at the end of October they are dark and it is a season for storms. At the beginning of the poem the narrator addresses Tam:

> … frae November till October,
> Ae market day thou wast nae sober.[40]

Burns thus places us at the beginning of the Celtic year. At the same time we are both in a pub in Ayr and in contact with a tradition which is two or three thousand years old.

Although set in Ayr and Alloway, the poem includes a few lines about Tam drinking in Kirkoswald. Kate reminds her husband:

> That at the Lord's house, even on Sunday,
> Thou drank wi' Kirkton Jean till Monday.[41]

This is Jean Kennedy, whose howff in Kirkoswald was called the Ladies' House after her and her sister. The area of Kirkoswald may have a connection with Halloween. On the rising ground above the village is a little hill, on the farm of Hallowshean – the Gaelic *sithean* pointing to an association with fairies (like Glen Shee in Perthshire) and 'hallow' possibly indicating the day on which the fairies met there (although the word may originally have been 'hollow'). At the beginning of 'Hallow-een', Burns names another fairy hill:

> Upon that night, when fairies light
> On Cassilis Downans dance.[42]

Halloween is the end of autumn, the end of the Celtic year, the beginning of the long tunnel of winter. It is a time for the meetings of witches and fairies, and for young humans to think about their future lives. Commerce and companionable conversation take place:

> When chapman billies leave the street,
> And drouthy neebors, neebors meet.[43]

NOTES

1 Robertson (1904), p. 7; Kinsley (1968), p. 195.
2 Ibid. (1904), p. 45; (1968), p. 282.
3 Child (1882-98), vol. 5, pp. 96-99.
4 Robertson (1904), p. 177; Kinsley (1968), p. 124.
5 Child (1882-98), vol. 3, pp. 299-301.
6 Robertson (1904), p. 110; Kinsley (1968), p. 116.
7 Ibid. (1904), p. 213; (1968), p. 16.
8 Ibid. (1904), p. 45; (1968), p. 282.
9 Ferguson and Roy (1985), vol. 2, p. 114.
10 Ibid., vol. 2, p. 265.
11 Hutton (1996), for festivals in the calendar.
12 Picken (1788), p. 14.
13 Robertson (1904), p. 106; Kinsley (1968), p. 165.
14 Ibid. (1904), p. 341; (1968), p. 13.
15 Ibid. (1904), p. 161; (1968), p. 85.
16 Old Statistical Account: Largs.
17 Robertson (1904), p. 51; Kinsley (1968), p. 103.
18 Mactaggart (1824), p. 171.
19 Edgar (1885-86), p. 148.
20 Letter from a Blacksmith (1759), p. 19.
21 Robertson (1904), p. 34; Kinsley (1968), p. 132.
22 Ibid. (1904), p. 34; (1968), p. 135.
23 Shakespeare: Hamlet, act 1, scene 5.
24 Robertson (1904), p. 37; Kinsley. (1968), p. 136.
25 Ibid. (1904), p. 38; (1968), p. 137.
26 Letter from a Blacksmith (1759), 14.
27 Brook (1906-07).
28 Luke 22:19.
29 Mayne (1836), p. 5.
30 Mackie (1896), pp. 18-20.
31 New Statistical Account: Dalry (Ayrshire).
32 Macfarlane (1906-08), vol. 3, p. 186.
33 Heron (1799), p. 14.
34 Robertson (1904), p. 19; Kinsley (1968), pp. 153-54.
35 Ibid. (1904), p. 560; (1968), pp. 153-54.
36 Ibid. (1904), p. 561; (1968), p. 155.
37 Ibid. (1904), p. 20; (1968), p. 155.
38 Ibid. (1904), p. 562; (1968), p. 160.
39 Ibid. (1904), p. 425; (1968), p. 808.
40 Ibid. (1904), p. 1; (1968), p. 558.
41 Ibid. (1904), p. 2; (1968), p. 558.
42 Ibid. (1904), p. 18; (1968), p. 152.
43 Ibid. (1904), p. 1; (1968), p. 557.

CHAPTER 8

Tam o' Shanter

BURNS wrote 'Tam o' Shanter' in the autumn and early winter of 1790, when the 31-year-old was at Ellisland. One starting point for examining the poem is Burns's friendship with the English antiquarian, Francis Grose [see *fig.* 1]. The two met when Grose was staying with his neighbours Elizabeth and Robert Riddell. Burns was impressed by him: 'He has mingled in all societies, & known every body.' Grose was a gross individual, low, squat and rotund, 'a fine fat fodgel wight' (*fodgel* meaning well-built). He said that his circumference was more than twice his height. Grose was a sociable man, pudgy and genial, a joker and porter-drinker. In the dark he explored the criminal slums of London, as Charles Dickens did later, and he assembled the language of the elusive world of thieves, and of his hard and hearty drinking friends, into *A Dictionary of the Vulgar Tongue* (1785): for example, to be hung was to 'kick the clouds'. Francis Grose died at dinner.

Grose and Burns had much in common: a convivial nature, humour, an intense awareness of the past and a wish to re-interpret it (Burns in song and Grose in his drawings and descriptions of old buildings). Burns once described Grose in action thus:

> *By some auld, houlet-haunted biggin,* [owl]
> *Or kirk deserted by its riggin',* [ridging, i.e. roof]
> *It's ten to ane ye'll find him snug in*

> *Some eldrich part,*
> *Wi' diels, they say, Lord save's! colleaguin'*
> *At some black art.*[1]

Does Burns mean himself as well as Grose? 'Black art' was the kind of expression Burns used to mean any kind of inspired, creative activity.

Grose was a member of a group with which Burns was familiar. Burns knew several of the key figures in the founding (1781) and development of the Society of Antiquaries of Scotland. Its Secretary was William Smellie, printer, publisher and editor of the *Encyclopedia Britannica* (1768-71), and of Buchan's *Domestic Medicine* (1769). He was also Burns's 'ancient, trusty, drouthy cronie', and fellow enthusiast for ribald verse. The President of the Antiquaries was the Earl of Buchan, who saw himself as a guardian of Scottish history, and the man who wrote to Burns to advise him to write in English rather than Scots. Another adviser on literary taste was Alexander Fraser Tytler; he, like Burns's publisher William Creech, was a keen antiquary. Grose was another.

As well as words, Grose collected objects. Burns told a friend, who was a numismatist, that Grose would give him items from his own collection:

> *So may ye get in glad possession,*
> *The coins o' Satan's coronation!*[2]

… that is, medals issued to celebrate his coronation. Grose also collected views in his published volumes, just as Burns helped George Thomson and James Johnson to assemble their collections of songs: indeed, Johnson's was called *The Scots Musical Museum*. Grose made a collection of advertising matter which he found ludicrous. Under the ironic title of *A Guide to Health, Beauty, Riches and Honour* (1783), he set out 108 advertisements printed over half a century which offered the services of matchmakers, dentists, wigmakers, moneylenders, astrologers, dancing masters and vendors of patent medicines.

Grose was robustly doubtful about the supernatural, saying that in the popular mind it was 'little less than atheism' to doubt ghost stories, even though the number of ghosts in churchyards seemed to be almost equal to the number of living parishioners. He summed up his view of apparitions by saying that if a drunken farmer, retiring from the market, fell from Old Dobbin and broke his neck, then that spot was ever after haunted.[3]

News of what Grose was doing arrived in Dumfries before Burns went to live at Ellisland. At the beginning of 1789 Grose's proposal to publish *The Antiquities of Scotland* was printed in the *Dumfries Weekly Journal* – the book would appear in 36 parts, each with four engraved views and a text. Each was to cost half-a-crown, making it £4-10/- for the entire series. In comparison, Burns's salary when he joined the excise was £4-3/4 a month. Grose asked for original drawings, plans of buildings, and information relating to castles, abbeys and ancient ruins. Having run short of money, he was setting himself up as a professional author and preparing for a major publishing effort: he announced his *Treatise on Ancient Armour and Military Antiquities*, which was also issued in parts.[4]

Burns suggested to Grose that Kirk Alloway should be included, although it was smaller and less distinguished than most of the buildings Grose drew and described [see *fig. 2*]. Grose agreed, provided Burns wrote a poem to be published in the *Antiquities*. In a letter Burns told Grose three versions of the story which was the intended basis for the poem. It has been said that they came from folk tradition, although they may have stemmed largely from Burns's imagination. Whatever their origin, he seems to have been working over the variations and trying out ideas on Grose.

The core of the story of Tam o' Shanter is the idea of a man going to an isolated building, seeing or hearing something fascinating but forbidden, and escaping. Another Ayrshire story involved the haunted tower at New Cumnock, where in the night a man heard beautiful music, and a rhythm like a dance. He put hand on the latch, there was a crash, the music stopped, and he found that the house was empty.[5] Burns often stayed nearby when he visited John Logan of Laight, so he may well have known the story.[6]

Grose himself knew a similar tale which did not involve the supernatural. One midnight a man was walking through Woolwich churchyard, when he heard singing. The church was dark and silent, but he found a group of drunken sailors carousing inside a family tomb. When the landlord of the alehouse in which they had been drinking had shut his door, the sailors had found this alternative venue, opened a coffin and put bread, cheese and beer in it.[7] So 'Tam o' Shanter' has links both with folk tales and with the kind of stories men tell in a tavern.

ROBERT BURNS AND THE HELLISH LEGION

We can also read 'Tam o' Shanter' as a parody of the Gothick novel. Horace Walpole in *The Castle of Otranto* (1764) had made the supernatural fashionable, with hauntings, black veils, skeletons and the rest. 'But are they [Gothick novels] all horrid, are you sure they are all horrid?' asks one of Jane Austen's heroines, newly installed in modish Bath. 'Yes, quite sure; for a particular friend of mine ... a sweet girl, one of the sweetest creatures in the world, has read every one of them.' Burns's poem has the same kind of subject, but it is set among country people.

The midnight meeting with supernatural content was a poetic vehicle for saying things which were difficult to say in the real world, and Burns was not the only poet to use it. His Irish contemporary, Brian Merriman, wrote 'The Midnight Court' in 1780. The action of Merriman's poem takes place in the village of Feakle, Co. Clare, probably where he was born. 'Tam o' Shanter' is set in Burns's birthplace. Both poets were farmers who left the land for the town; Merriman to become a teacher of mathematics. Both, during their farming days, won prizes for growing flax (Burns while he was at Lochlea). Merriman's poem describes the pressure on young people to marry someone who is much older and wealthier, and is sympathetic to women who have borne illegitimate children; it is fantastic and realistic at the same time. Finally, 'The Midnight Court' is a humorous poem, like 'Tam o' Shanter'.

We can now go through 'Tam o' Shanter', looking at how it stems from the culture of the people, and also seeing it to some extent as a present for Francis Grose, in recognition of his enthusiasms.[8]

* * *

When chapman billies leave the street,
And drouthy neibors, neibors meet.
As market-days are wearing late
An' folk begin to tak the gate.[9]

It is a quiet evening at the end of the weekly market in a medium-sized town. There is a sense of dispersal, of a new social pattern for the next few hours. We also learn later that this particular day is Halloween. If Burns's 'Halloween' is about people, and in particular their hope for the future, 'Tam' is concerned with the discovery of the other side, the supernatural, the hidden and the subconscious.

The poem begins when Tam is at an inn, 'Fast by an ingle, bleezing finely'. In 1770 there were 48 alehouses in Ayr, each one a room with a fire, a barrel and a bottle, and a warm, familiar friendliness. The fire was probably of coal, from one of the pits near the burgh, and it suggests the Hallowmas *bleeze*, and the drinkers who are *bleezin* drunk. There is a comfortable reality in the scene.

It is far from the first time Tam has sat drinking with his friends [see *fig.* 19]. His wife Kate told him:

> *That ilka melder, wi' the miller,*
> *Thou sat as lang as thou had siller;*
> *That every naig was ca'd a shoe on,*
> *The smith and thee gat roarin' fou on.*[10]

There are five decorated headstones in the kirkyard at Alloway, and three of them are for a miller, a smith and a farmer, like Tam. Is this a coincidence? Perhaps, but they were the three principal activities for men in the parish. Allan Ramsay's 'Christ's Kirk on the Green' is another poem involving pleasure and an old kirk: it describes a country festival beside the parish church. In Ramsay's poem, a souter [shoemaker], miller and smith are dining together in an inn:

> *... e'en tho' Auld Nick*
> *Shou'd tempt their wives to scald*
> *Them for't neist day.*[11]

When Tam reaches home he knows he is going to hear a sermon which would be worthy of Black Jock Russell. Kate is already preparing like a preacher before Communion:

> *Gathering her brows like gathering storm,*
> *Nursing her wrath to keep it warm.*[12]

When Burns says that she

> *... prophesied that, late or soon,*
> *Thou would be found deep drown'd in Doon.*[13]

he makes the connection with the Auld Lichts and their prophecies of doom. These lines take us into the world of the Devil and witches, Hell and damnation, the Auld Licht vision of this life and the next.

Tam's pleasures in life are also traditional: 'And aye the ale was growing better.'[14] Ale was the old drink; whisky was new and perhaps fashionable for ambitious young men, like Robert Burns.

* * *

Tam sets off from Ayr on his grey mare Meg, who may be a version of the horse Maggie in 'The Auld Farmer's New Year Salutation':

When thou was corn't, an' I was mellow,
We took the road aye like a swallow.[15]

The grey horse appears often in folklore. The Laird of Coul rode one, and so did Tam Lin. In a tale from Nithsdale, a young man was be-witched into being a grey mare for a carlin, taking her to the witches' tryst at Locharbriggs.[16] A 'grey mare' was, in London slang (according to Grose's *Dictionary*), a domineering wife, like Tam's; and in the poem he starts off in the saddle, but it is the grey horse which will get him out of trouble and deliver him back to his spouse.

Professor James Kinsley, editor of the standard edition of Burns's poems and songs, argued that the route from Ayr to Alloway was, at the time of the poem, closer to the shore than it is now, and this makes sense of the order in which Tam passed various landmarks. However, Roy's great map of Scotland, which was made just before Burns was born, shows the present road alignment, as does the Armstrongs' map (1775), so here we will assume that it is the line that Tam followed [see *fig.* 24].

For Burns, the route must have had an emotional content. It was the road along which he took the corpse of his father to be buried at Alloway. It was a couple of hundred yards from the spot on Ayr moor where David Edwards's bones had hung in the gibbet. Edwards had gone to the gallows a few months before Robert Burns was born, and his bones were still on display 20 years later, so that every journey the boy made into Ayr from Alloway or Mount Oliphant went past the skeleton. Mure of Auchendrane's agents murdered Thomas Kennedy of Colzean on the same road. All this was in the rustling of autumn's last leaves.

The wind blew as 'twad blawn its last;

The rattling show'rs rose on the blast;
The speedy gleams the darkness swallow'd;
Loud, deep, and lang, the thunder bellow'd:
That night, a child might understand,
The Deil had business on his hand.[17]

Burns said that he liked to walk on the sheltered side of a wood, and 'hear the stormy wind howling among the trees, and raving over the plain'. It 'was something which exalts me, something which enraptures me'.[18] Here he is making a directly emotional response to nature, engaging with it, allowing himself to be taken over by it. The imaginative Burns is able to enjoy the strength of the weather, but Tam cannot.

As he rode, Tam found himself in direct contact with the elements which make up nature – earth, air, water and fire, the last in the form of lightning:

Tam skelpit on thro' dub and mire,
Despising wind, and rain, and fire.[19]

The presence of large quantities of all four elements shows how extreme the situation is. The whole cosmos seems to be against Tam. The simple words Burns uses indicate that he is telling us about Tam's feelings. William Shakespeare once addressed a storm thus:

You cataracts and hurricanoes spout
Till you have drench'd our steeples drown'd the cocks.[20]

This is a disaster, a terrible ending to the lives of families and village communities. In comparison, Tam's experience of being wet, cold, frightened and alone is personal. He has, however, his knowledge of bogles, kelpies and unnamable horrors to keep him company. Tam rides through a topography of terrors:

By this time he was cross the ford,
Where in the snaw the chapman smoor'd; [was smothered]
And past the birks and meikle stane,
Where drunken Charlie brak's neck-bane;
And thro' the whins, and by the cairn,
Where hunters fand the murder'd bairn.[21]

Roads were places where things happened – where those with worn-out clothes were chilled, where those whose minds were elsewhere might stumble in the ruts, particularly if the clachan yill [village ale] had made them canty, and along which the desperate made their flight. But these were solid human experiences, while Tam is about to lose contact with the real world.

From wind and water Burns moves back to fire.

> *When, glimmering thro' the groaning trees,*
> *Kirk-Alloway seem'd in a bleeze.*[22]

Bleeze is a rich word. It relates to holidays that were generally celebrated by bonfires, and it was applied specifically to one of the quarter days, Candlemas: we have already met the 'Candlemas *bleeze*'. A *bleeze* was a warning beacon, and also a signal for a ferry, to say that a boat was wanted on the opposite side. 'To bleeze a burn' means to carry a burning torch to attract salmon towards a fisherman armed with a spear-like leister. Corn is 'in a bleeze' when it is ripe and ready for harvest. A *bleeze* is not merely alight – it is alive and beckoning, and when you see one, something is about to happen.

At midsummer 1787 Burns walked the seven miles from Edinburgh to see Roslin's romantic castle at dawn. He was with Alexander Nasmyth, the portrait painter, who made a number of sketches of the poet while they were there, which he used when he made his famous portrait. Roslin has links with 'Tam o' Shanter'. The castle has a ghostly black dog, possibly a relative of the 'towzie tyke', who Tam is about to see. Above the castle is the most extraordinary building in Scotland, the hyper-decorated and profusely symbolic late medieval Rosslyn chapel, in which the stone has been carved as if it were butter. The castle was the stronghold of the St Clair family, one of whom fought at Bannockburn and died fighting the Moors when the heart of Robert Bruce was carried into battle. (This would have satisfied Burns's feeling for history.) Before one of the St Clair family died, it was said that Rosslyn chapel itself seemed to be in a blaze. Grose wrote about this in his *Antiquities of Scotland*, and it is possible that he had the information from Burns.[23]

Back in Alloway, however, Tam approaches the kirk:

> *Thro' ilka bore the beams were glancing,*
> *And loud resounded mirth and dancing.*[24]

'And, vow! Tam saw an unco sight!' [25]

There sat auld Nick, in shape o' beast —
A touzie tyke, black, grim and large!
To gie them music was his charge:
He screw'd the pipes and gart them skirl,
Till roof and rafters a' did dirl. [26]

Tam sees what an Auld Licht adherent would expect to see – the Devil in the form of a black dog, mentioned before in Scottish witch trials. But what is unfamiliar is the sight of the 'Earl of Hell' having fun [see *fig. 8*]:

As Tammie glowr'd, amaz'd, and curious,
The mirth and fun grew fast and furious:
The piper loud and louder blew;
The dancers quick and quicker flew;
They reel'd, they set, they cross'd, they cleekit,
Till ilka carlin swat and reekit,
And coost her duddies to the wark,
And linket at it in her sark! [27]

James Kinsley has pointed out that the verbs which label the witches' actions form a pattern: *reel'd – set – cross'd – cleekit – swat – reekit*. They have the initial letters RSCCSR, which may be interpreted as the scheme of a reel. [28] Burns is very far from showing all his tricks openly.

The witches' activity can also be related to the Dance of Death, a strange and powerful medieval image, of skeletons leading living people towards the grave. In Kirk Alloway the living are dancing and the skeletons are watching. Burns's witches are performing the dance of life.

The witches' dance sounds, too, like the impassioned antics of Alexander Moodie when he is preaching in 'The Holy Fair':

Now meekly calm, now wild in wrath,
He's stampin', an' he's jumpin'!
His lengthen'd chin, his turned-up snout,
His eldritch squeal an' gestures,
O how they fire the heart devout,
Like cantharadian plaisters,
   On sic a day! [29]

His face is diabolic, and he is squealing like the Devil's bagpipes. We can see how the Devil leads and excites the witches too.

What Tam sees is a witches' sabbath. On Halloween the witches meet the Devil, and this explains Tam's fear of being caught by bogles, and may have contributed to his reluctance to leave Ayr, for he knew that supernatural things might happen. An Ayrshire novelist once said of Halloween that 'The de'il at other times gi'es, it's said, his agents a mutchkin o' mischief, but on this night it's thought they hae a *chappin*'.[30] A *choppin* is a measure twice the size of the mutchkin.

Burns must have been familiar with all of this: the tradition in lower Nithsdale was that local witches met on Halloween on top of Lochar-briggs Hill, five miles from Ellisland.

The witches' dance can also be seen as a harvest festival, a kirn, a celebration of the successful gathering of the year's crop, which has been laid out in the kirk. Burns talks of the kirn in 'The Twa Dogs'.

> *As bleak-faced Hallowmas returns*
> *They get the jovial, rantin' kirns,*
> *When rural life, o' every station*
> *Unite in common recreation;*
> *Love blinks, Wit slaps, an' social Mirth*
> *Forgets there's Care upo' the earth.*[31]

At Alloway Tam sees a celebration of a successful summer of evil, garnished with murder weapons and skeletons. The decoration of the kirk included bizarre homeliness:

> *Coffins stood round like open presses,*
> *That shaw'd the dead in their last dresses;*
> *And by some devilish cantraip sleight*
> *Each in its cauld hand held a light.*[32]

The dead have become a macabre version of the *peer-man*, a wooden stand which held a fir-candle to light a winter room.

Tam saw more human remains:

> *... Tam was able*
> *To note upon the haly table*
> *A murderer's banes in gibbet-airns;*

Twa span-lang, wee, unchristen'd bairns;
A thief, new-cutted frae a rape —
Wi' his last gasp his gab did gape.[33]

The murderer's bones, of course, are those of David Edwards. The Devil is also behaving as an apothecary, showing off the corpses which are the raw materials for making poisons, with which he will cause more trouble.

In the exhibition are 'Twa span-lang, wee unchristen'd bairns'. Before babies were baptised they were vulnerable to the attentions of witches and fairies, and in this period children were not full members of society. It had once been common to bury them in a separate part of the churchyard from those who had been christened. In Ramsay's 'The Gentle Shepherd', Bauldy (short for Archibald) says of the local witch:

She can o'er cast the Night, and cloud the Moon
And mak diels obedient to her Crune,
At Midnight hours, o'er the Kirk-yards she raves,
And howks unchristen'd weans out of their Graves.[34]

One of the prose stories about Kirk Alloway which Burns told Grose had a central figure who was a farm servant who had been in Ayr to collect ploughing irons from the smith. At the kirk he sees a stew of heads of unchristened children and the limbs of malefactors, a soup of innocence and cruelty.

Next Tam sees an exotic selection of murder implements:

Five tomahawks, wi' blude red rusted;
Five scymitars, wi' murder crusted;
A garter, which a babe had strangled;
A knife, a father's throat had mangled,
Whom his ain son o' life bereft —
The grey hairs yet stack to the heft;
Wi' mair of horrible and awfu',
Which even to name wad be unlawfu'.[35]

The 'scymitars' are the weapons of the infidel Mohammedans, making a link with the Devil under the name of 'Auld Mahoun'. Overall, it is a collection like Grose's 'auld nick-nackets'. It is an image of the Society of Antiquaries, as it would have been seen by a roistering member of the Caledonian Hunt Club. And it has something to do with John Hornbook's armoury of 'saws and whittles' with which he tried to cure people.

One of the goals of the Antiquaries was to assemble a museum of ancient things and list them as a preliminary way of understanding them. A generation before, the Swedish naturalist Carl Linné had produced his system for naming plants and animals, and catalogues that attempted to cover the whole of the natural world, species by species. Information, when written or in the form of physical objects, was increasingly becoming structured: like Sinclair's *Statistical Account of Scotland*; like the copy of *A Select Collection of Original Scottish Airs*, for which Burns had written so many songs, given by the editor to the Society of Antiquaries [see *fig. 5*]; like the alphabetical glossary at the end of the Kilmarnock edition; like the criminal relics laid out in Kirk Alloway.

This assemblage of several kinds of weapon of the same kind may also be linked to the arrangement of symbols in heraldry, a subject rich in strange beasts and archaic weaponry.

Burns was advised to cut four lines from the poem. They were a continuation of the catalogue:

> *Three lawyers' tongues turn'd inside out,*
> *Wi' lies seam'd like a beggar's clout;*
> *Three priests' hearts rotten, black as muck,*
> *Lay stinkin vile in every neuk.*[36]

If the tongues were 'seam'd like a beggar's clout', then they were patched. However, since they were tongues they may link to leather rather than cloth, and shoes have tongues. One of the techniques of shoemaking is to create concealed joins between pieces of leather, or metaphorically to hide the lies. This meaning is reinforced by the word 'seam'd', indicating that the lawyers' words seemed to be true: Burns did not used the most obvious Scots word, *steek'd*.

'Seam'd' or 'seemed' – the idea is growing in the poem that all is not what it seems. The easy way to look at 'Tam o' Shanter' is to regard it as an alcoholic phantasmagoria, the dream of a drunk; but the variety of cultural references that can be drawn from it suggest that Burns is up to something, but he is not telling us what it is.

At this point in the story Tam loses control and shouts, 'Weel done, Cutty-sark!' [see *fig.* 11]:

And in an instant all was dark!
And scarcely had he Maggie rallied,
When out the hellish legion sallied.

Burns then makes a comparison with boys attacking beehives:

As bees bizz out wi' angry fyke, [excitement]
When plundering herds assail their byke.[37] [hive]

The herd lads who rip open a hive in search of sweetness are destroying a community, so the bees are angry with good cause. Tam is threatening the witches' pleasure. The Kirk regarded dancing as sinful, and that is how Tam would have seen it; but it is unmistakable that the witches are having fun and, like the bees, they are sociable.

In a few more instants, horse and rider are on the brig. To save Tam's life, Maggie has had to gallop the distance between the kirk and the bridge, in reality not much more than 200 yards.

At the kirk, and during the race to the brig, Tam has the chance on Halloween to cross to another world. The man in 'Allison Gross' and Tam Lin himself take the chance, but the terrified farmer does not. The rituals in Burns's 'Halloween' are about finding a mate, and there in the dance is Nannie waiting for him. Can you imagine Burns missing the opportunity to dance with an attractive woman who is wearing nothing but a sark? '*Tam* tint [lost] his reason a' thegither',[38] and instead of a life full of possibilities and dancing, he flees to his wife and the safe and familiar fears of the Auld Licht.

We can compare Tam's decision with another encounter between a man and a group of witches – the one in 'Macbeth' [see *fig.* 6]. In Shakespeare's play, Macbeth seeks supernatural advice as to how to act. The witches make their predictions, and the future king goes off with a course of action before him. Unlike Tam, he allows the witches to change his life, though they also point the way to his early death. Unlike Burns, Macbeth hungers for political power, not the ability to use his imagination.

Daniel Defoe described the Brig o' Doon as 'a bridge of one arch, the longest I ever saw, much larger than the Rialto at Venice'.[39] In the eighteenth century it was an impressive structure. 'Here, Doon pour'd down his far-fetched floods' and the flood carried memories of the country it drained, the wet hillsides round Dalmellington where the soldiers had chased, caught and killed Covenanters. It was a well-watered country, of mosses and slaps – never far from a tumbling burn or scouring river, and routes across the land were fixed by fords and bridges. When Kennedy of Bargany was riding to his death in 1601, he stopped at the Brig and told his men that if they wished they could ride away and leave him to his fate. A bridge is a place where decisions are made and where decisive actions take place.

The running water is also a barrier to the witches. It is not like the earth, which gives life and strength. The cold water protects, and in this case saves Tam's life. However, its coldness means that it is unemotional. It is a slosh of sobering water which makes him his old self once again.

As Maggie crosses the bridge, Nannie pulls off her tail.

> *The carlin claught her by the rump* [seized]
> *And left poor Maggie scarce a stump.*[40]

The Roman idea of Fortune was that she was a naked old woman, covered with oil, who had a single hair in the middle of her forehead. 'To seize Fortune by the forelock' was to take hold of that hair, and so gain Fortune. After the first chance to catch her, however, the hair was no longer there – Fortune could be grappled with, but not caught. She sounds something like the dancing, sweaty witches. It is the lively Nannie who takes hold of Fortune, not in the form of a hair but as Meg's tail, opening the way to a successful career as a witch:

> *For mony a beast to dead she shot,*
> *An' perish'd mony a bonnie boat.*[41]

And of course, Fortune is the concern of the young people on Halloween seeking images of their partners in life: they were 'fortune'-telling.

How did Tam get himself into this situation? People who were going to take communion at a holy fair [*fig.* 20] received a token giving them admission to the ceremony [*fig.* 10]. The coins Tam gave the land-lady of the inn in Ayr were the tokens that allowed him to enter into the experience which is told in the poem. The communion token, however, only admits the individual to the ceremony, and not to the state of grace.

This can only be achieved if communion is taken in the right frame of mind. So Tam is allowed to experience the sights at the kirk, but if he is going to participate, and start a different life, he has to enter the building and join the dance. Even though he is drunk, to use a modern expression, he bottles it.

There is a Scots proverb: 'it is dear bought honey that is lickt off a thorn.' A common theme in folk tales is the hero who has a life-threatening experience, but survives it and gains something precious, such as treasure, a wife, or wisdom. So what has Tam gained? If riding for his life was to Tam like licking a thorn, what was the honey? It is difficult to see any reward for him. He has cattle, his wife makes butter, and Nannie has had a good look at him and can make the thuggish threat: I know where you live. For today, Tam has escaped, but he will continue to be afraid of boglework and witchery. He has had his pleasure in looking lecherously at Nannie; now, in his mind, he is going to pay for it.

David Daiches has called the last six lines of the poem 'a mock moral', a misleading simplification.

> *Now, wha this tale o' truth shall read,*
> *Ilk man and mother's son, take heed:*
> *Whene'er to drink you are inclin'd,*
> *Or cutty-sarks run in your mind,*
> *Think, ye may buy the joys o'er dear,*
> *Remember Tam o' Shanter's mare.*[42]

We can perhaps go further. Burns is saying the opposite of what he means; he is asserting the importance of pleasure in human existence, and the need for freedom in order to be creative.

The Devil can been seen in two ways. He is seen as evil by the traditionalists like Jock Russell and Tam, but to Burns he is a creative spirit, He is the same figure as the poet in 'The Jolly Beggars': except that when Burns wrote the 'anarchist cantata'[43] in 1785 he had been half observer and half participant, and his poetry had not been printed, whereas by 1790 he had advanced to presiding over the revels. The witches dance to his tunes as, in reality, did the women with whom Burns had affairs.

The creative Devil plays music, and he plays in a more general way, seeking and seeing alternatives. After he has played, something new has appeared, even if it is just a teasing memory. Thomas Stothard's painting

of 'The Deil's Awa' wi' the Exciseman' (c.1814) [see *fig. 26*], which illustrates Burns's song, shows the joy of the people at the removal to Hell
of a man who has plagued them. Every figure but one is smiling or
laughing, and the Devil is the hero who makes it possible for everyone
to enjoy themselves. The scene is outside an inn, where the Exciseman
has been checking the stocks of drink.

The world as we know it depends on the existence of Satan. But for
him, Adam and Eve would still be living in the timeless innocence of the
Garden of Eden. Satan gave self-awareness to humankind. God made
man and woman, but Satan made them recognisably (and touchingly)
human.

Poet William Montgomerie wrote of the Devil in 'Tam o' Shanter':

> *He is the part of the human personality suppressed by Calvinism,*
> *Burns the poet and fornicator, the creator of music, the inspirer of*
> *dancing, summing up in himself all the elements in the Scotsman*
> *that the Kirk, unable to destroy them, for they are an essential part*
> *of our nature, has suppressed. He is 'a touzie tyke', the animal in*
> *all of us.*[44]

Montgomerie is right, but here we are moving towards a more specific
conclusion: the 'touzie tyke' is a source of creativity, for he looks beyond
the expected, the conventional and the taboo, to see the surprising, the
shape which does not fit the pattern, and the layers of meaning below the
surface.

In an elated mood Burns wrote from Dumfries to his friend Bob
Ainslie in Edinburgh about the writer's need for freedom and creative
disorder. A *spunkie* is a will-o'-the-wisp, and the poet imagines his
thoughts following its light:

> *SPUNKIE – thou shalt henceforth be my Symbol, Signature, &*
> *Tutelary Genius! Like thee, hap-step-&-lowp, here-awa-there-*
> *awa, higgelty-piggelty, pell-mell, hither-&-yon, ram-stam, happy-*
> *go-lucky, up-tails-a'-by-the light-o'-the-moon, has been, is, &*
> *shall be, my progress through the mosses & moors of this vile,*
> *bleak, barren wilderness of a life of ours.*[45]

Burns was born in earth, and now his element was fire. A *spunk*, as Dr
Johnson recorded, was a match, a small piece of wood which had been

dipped in sulphur. A more sophisticated version was later sold as the Lucifer. This kind of *spunk* was largely urban: in the country *spunks* were rather larger pieces of Scots pine that burned well because of the resin in them, and one of the ways of holding them was to use a *peerman*.[46] Resin, too, is the rosin for the bow of the fiddle which the Devil is playing for the witches' reels.

A *spunkie* was something sparkling. Burns used the word as a metaphor for whisky:

> But gie me just a true good fallow
>   Wi' right ingine,
> And spunkie ance to mak us mellow,
>   And then we'll shine![47]

Burns's ideal companion is in fact himself, sociable, loyal, and 'Wi' right ingine'. Allan Ramsay referred to 'Old Chaucer, Bard of vast Ingine'[48] – deep originality, resourcefulness and invention. Burns was the same. 'Tam o' Shanter', in this reading, is about the need to escape from the structured, over-ruled orthodoxy of traditional Calvinism, to allow energy and creativity to flow in a way which the Auld Lichts regarded as sinful.

When Burns says 'And then we'll shine', he seems to say that all the people of Scotland can be like this – if we are sociable, if we stick together, we can make the world a better place and have some fun along the way. This brings us to an irony, for Burns could stand up to those in religious authority, but not to political powers. He sympathised with the equality and fairness which he believed would emerge from the French Revolution; but when he said so, his masters in the Excise threatened to punish or expel him, and Burns chose to conform.

'Tam o' Shanter' is for Burns a personal poem, based on the hamlet in which he was born, and the kirkyard where his father, who had taught him so much and enabled so much more, lay buried. Like 'The Holy Fair', it is about escaping from convention and the dour crows of one kind of Calvinism, but it is also about a larger subject. The poem signposts the difficult path to creativity in a world of Tams and Kates, and in that sense it is autobiographical. As well as the explicitly supernatural, it is also implicitly supernatural; for the other world is the source of creativity, of the unknown, of the poem which has not yet been written.

To conclude, we can return to 'The Jolly Beggars', in whose final section the poet sings his praise of freedom from the Auld Lichts, and from all forms of convention and possession, in a song with a memorably mocking final word [see *fig. 7*]. He writes of love, but he writes too in praise of the imagination, of the liberty to write and to communicate with his friends as they go through life together:

> *With the ready trick and fable*
>> *Round we wander all the day;*
> *And at night, in barn or stable,*
>> *Hug our doxies on the hay.*
>
> *Does the train-attended CARRIAGE*
>> *Thro' the country lighter rove?*
> *Does the sober bed of MARRIAGE*
>> *Witness brighter scenes of love?*
>
> *Life is all a VARIORUM,*
>> *We regard not how it goes;*
> *Let them cant about DECORUM,*
>> *Who have character to lose.*
>
> *Here's to BUDGETS, BAGS and WALLETS!*
>> *Here's to all the wandering train!*
> *Here's to our ragged BRATS and CALLETS!* [wenches]
>> *One and all, cry out, AMEN!*[49]

NOTES

1 Robertson (1904), p. 127; Kinsley (1968), p. 494.
2 *Ibid.* (1904), p. 526; (1968), p. 565.
3 Grose (1787), p. 3.
4 *Dumfries Weekly Journal*, January 1789.
5 Steven (1899), p. 86.
6 *Ibid.*, p. 94.
7 Grose (1796), pp. 182-83.
8 For other interpretations of the poem see, for example, Daiches (1966), pp. 249-60; Crawford (2009), pp. 327-30.
9 Robertson (1904), p. 1; Kinsley (1968), p. 557.
10 *Ibid.* (1904), p. 1; (1968), p. 558.
11 Ramsay (1945-74), vol. 1, p. 73.
12 Robertson (1904), p. 1; Kinsley (1968), p. 557.
13 *Ibid.* (1904), p. 2; (1968), p. 558.
14 *Ibid.* (1904); *ibid.* (1968).
15 *Ibid.* (1904), p. 107; (1968), p. 166.

16 Cromek (1880).
17 Robertson (1904), p. 3; Kinsley (1968), p. 559.
18 Burns (1872), p. 11.
19 Robertson (1904), p. 3; Kinsley (1968), p. 559.
20 Shakespeare: *King Lear*, act 3, scene 2.
21 Robertson (1904), p. 3; Kinsley (1968), p. 560.
22 *Ibid.* (1904); (1968).
23 Grose (1789-91), vol. 1, p. 47.
24 Robertson (1904), p. 3; Kinsley (1968), p. 560.
25 *Ibid.* (1904), p. 4; (1968).
26 *Ibid.* (1904); (1968), p. 561.
27 *Ibid.* (1904); (1968), p. 561-62.
28 Kinsley (1968), p. 1362.
29 Robertson (1904), p. 34; Kinsley (1968), p. 132-33.
30 Galt (1823), ch. 22.
31 Robertson (1904), p. 41; Kinsley (1968), p. 141.
32 *Ibid.* (1904), p. 4; (1968), p. 561.
33 *Ibid.* (1904); (1968).
34 Ramsay (1945-74), vol. 2, p. 129.
35 Robertson (1904), p. 4; Kinsley (1968), p. 561.
36 *Ibid.* (1904), p. 557; (1968), p. 561, note.
37 *Ibid.* (1904), p. 5; (1968), p. 563.
38 *Ibid.* (1904); (1968).
39 Defoe (1968), p. 601.
40 Robertson (1904), p. 6; Kinsley (1968), p. 564.
41 *Ibid.* (1904), p. 5; (1968), p. 564.
42 *Ibid.* (1904), p. 6; (1968).
43 Daiches (1966), p. 196.
44 Montgomerie (1947), pp. 70-84, quoting from p. 79.
45 Ferguson and Roy (1985), vol. 2, p. 174.
46 Anderson (1794), p. 30.
47 Robertson (1904), p. 229; Kinsley (1968), p. 221.
48 Ramsay (1945-74), vol. 2, p. 179.
49 Robertson (1904), p. 16; Kinsley (1968), pp. 208-09.

Select Bibliography

ABERCROMBY, JOHN (1894): 'An unpublished Scottish lullaby', in *Folklore*, 5, p. 236.

ADAIR, JAMES MAKITTRICK (1790): *Anecdotes of the Life of a Medical Character* (London).

AITON, WILLIAM (1811): *General View of the Agriculture of the County of Ayr* (Glasgow).

A. M. (1820): 'Apparitions of the Devil', in *Edinburgh Magazine*, October, pp. 339-43.

_____ (1820): 'Historical notices of the popular traditions of ... Teviotdale', in *Edinburgh Magazine*, February, pp. 133-36; April, pp. 342-48 and June, pp. 533-36.

ANDERSON, JAMES (1794): *A Practical Treatise on Peat Moss* (Edinburgh).

BANKS, M. M. (1935): 'Tangled thread mazes', in *Folklore*, 46, pp. 78-80.

_____ (1937-41): *British Calendar Customs – Scotland*, 3 vols (London).

_____ (1939): 'Scottish lore of earth, its fruits, and the plough', in *Folklore*, 50, pp. 12-32.

BLACK, GEORGE (1892-93): 'Scottish charms and amulets', in *Proceedings of the Society of Antiquaries of Scotland*, 37, pp. 433-526.

BRIGGS, KATHERINE M. (1970): *A Dictionary of British Folk-Tales*, 4 vols (London).

BROOK, A. J. S. (1906-07): 'Communion tokens of the Established Church of Scotland', in *Proceedings of the Society of Antiquaries of Scotland*, 41, pp. 453-604.

BURKE, PETER (1978): *Popular Culture in Early Modern Europe*, 2nd edition (London).

BURNETT, JOHN (2007-08): 'Drinking goats' whey: an eighteenth-century cure in Scotland', *Folk Life*, 46, pp. 131-42.

BURNES, WILLIAM (1875): *A Manual of Religious Belief* (Kilmarnock).

BURNS, ROBERT (1808): *The Poetical Works of Robert Burns* (Alnwick).

_____ (1872): *Robert Burns' Common Place Book* (Edinburgh).

_____ (1904): *Poetical Works of Robert Burns* (see Robertson [1904]).

_____ (1968): *Poems* (see Kinsley [1968]).

_____ (1985): *Letters* (see Ferguson and Roy [1985]).

CAMPBELL, GEORGE (1787): *Poems on Several Occasions* (Kilmarnock).

CHAMBERS, ROBERT (1858): *Popular Rhymes of Scotland*, 3rd edition (Edinburgh).

CHEAPE, HUGH (2008): '"Charms against witchcraft": magic and mischief in museum collections', in Julian Goodare, Lauren Martin and Joyce Miller (eds) (2008): *Witchcraft and Belief in Early Modern Scotland* (Basingstoke, London), pp. 227-48.

CHEVIOT, ANDREW (1896): *Proverbs, Proverbial Expressions, and Popular Rhymes of Scotland* (Paisley).

CHILD, FRANCIS (1882-98): *The English and Scottish Popular Ballads*, 5 vols (Boston).

'CLAUDERO' [i.e. JAMES WILSON] (1771): *Miscellanies, in Prose and Verse* (Edinburgh).

COCK, JAMES (1806): *Simple Strains* (Aberdeen).

COWAN, EDWARD J. (1997): 'Burns and superstition', in Kenneth Simpson (ed.), *Love and Liberty: Robert Burns, a Bicentenary Celebration*, pp. 229-38 (East Linton).

_____ and MARK PATERSON (2007): *Folk in Print: Scotland's Chapbook Heritage, 1750-1850* (Edinburgh).

_____ and LIZANNE HENDERSON (2002): 'The last of the witches? The survival of Scottish witch belief', in Julian Goodare (ed.), *The Scottish Witch-Hunt in Context* (Manchester), pp. 198-217.

CRAWFORD, ROBERT (2009): *The Bard: Robert Burns, a Biography* (London).

CREECH, WILLIAM (1791): *Edinburgh Fugitive Pieces* (Edinburgh).

CROMEK, ROBERT HARTLEY (1808): *Select Scottish Songs ... with critical observations and biographical notices by Robert Burns* (London).

_____ (1810): *Reliques of Robert Burns* (London).

_____ (1880): *Remains of Nithsdale and Galloway Song* (Paisley).

DAICHES, DAVID (1966): *Robert Burns: the Poet*, 2nd edition.

DAVIDSON, DAVID (1789): *Thoughts on the Seasons* (London).

DEFOE, DANIEL (1724-26): *A Tour Through the Whole Island of Great Britain* (London 1724-26; Harmondsworth 1986).

DEVINE, T. M. (1994): *The Transformation of Rural Scotland* (Edinburgh).

_____ (1999): *Scottish Nation 1700-2000* (London).

DICK, OLIVER LAWSON (1972): *Aubrey's Brief Lives* (Harmondsworth).

DOUGLAS, NORMAN (1917): *South Wind* (London 1917; Harmondsworth, 1976).

EDGAR, ANDREW (1885-86): *Old Church Life in Scotland*, 2 vols (Paisley).

EVANS, JOHN (1872): *Ancient Stone Implements* (London).

EWING, J. C. (1919): 'Authorship of the "Verses on the Destruction of the Woods near Drumlanrig"', *Burns Chronicle*, 28, pp. 108-10.

FENTON, ALEXANDER (2000): *Scottish Country Life*, 2nd edition (East Linton).

_____ (2007): *The Food of the Scots* (Edinburgh).

FERGUSON, J. DE LANCY and G. ROSS ROY (eds) (1985): *The Letters of Robert Burns*, 2nd edition (Oxford).

FERGUSSON, ALEXANDER (1886): *The Laird of Lag* (Edinburgh).

FERGUSSON, ROBERT (1807): *Works* (London).

GALT, JOHN (1823/1984): *Ringan Gilhaize* (Edinburgh).

GRANT, W. and D. MURISON (eds) (1931-76): *The Scottish National Dictionary*, 10 vols (Edinburgh).

GREGOR, WALTER (1898): 'Fourth report on folklore in Scotland', in *Report of the Sixty-seventh Meeting of the British Association for the Advancement of Science held in Toronto in August 1897*, pp. 456-500.

GROSE, FRANCIS (1787): *A Provincial Glossary* (London).

_____ (1789-91): *Antiquities of Scotland*, 2 vols. (London).

_____ (1796): *The Olio, being a Collection of Essays*, 2nd edition (London).

HAMILTON, DAVID (1981): *The Healers: a History of Medicine in Scotland* (Edinburgh).

The Harangues, or Speeches, of Several Celebrated Quack-Doctors (London, 1762).

HENDERSON, JOHN (1812): *General View*

of the Agriculture of the County of
Caithness (London).

HENDERSON, LIZANNE and EDWARD J.
COWAN (2001): Scottish Fairy Belief:
a History (East Linton).

HERD, DAVID (1869): Ancient and
Modern Scottish Songs, Heroic
Ballads, &c. (Glasgow).

HERON, ROBERT (1797): Memoir of the
Life of the Late Robert Burns
(Edinburgh).

_____ (1799): Observations made in
a Journey through the Western
Counties of Scotland, 2 vols (Perth).

HEWAT, KIRKWOOD (1894): A Little
Scottish World (Kilmarnock).

HOGG, JAMES (1807): The Mountain
Bard (Edinburgh).

_____ (1995): The Shepherd's
Calendar (Edinburgh).

HUTTON, RICHARD (1996): Stations of
the Sun (Oxford).

JOHNSON, SAMUEL (1775): Journey to
the Western Islands of Scotland
(London).

JOHNSTONE, WILLIAM (1867): The Bard
and the Belted Knight (Edinburgh).

KINSLEY, JAMES (ed.) (1968): The Poems
and Songs of Robert Burns, 3 vols
(Oxford).

LAMB, H. H. (1982): Climate, History
and the Modern World (London).

Letter from a Blacksmith to the
Ministers and Elders of the Church
of Scotland (1759) (Dublin).

LOCH, DAVID (1778): Tour Through
Most of the Working Towns
and Villages of Scotland (Edinburgh).

MACFARLANE, WALTER (1906-08):
Geographical Collections Relating
to Scotland, 3 vols (Edinburgh).

MACKAY, JAMES A. (1992): Burns:
A Biography of Robert Burns
(Edinburgh).

MACKIE, CHARLES (1913): Dumfries
and Galloway Notes and Queries
(Dumfries).

MACKIE, DAVID (1896): Ayrshire Village
Sketches (Kilmarnock).

MacPHERSON, J. M. (1929): Primitive
Beliefs in the North-East of Scotland
(London).

MacTAGGART, JOHN (1824, rep. 1981):
The Scottish Gallovidian Encyclopedia.

MAYNE, JOHN (1836): The Siller Gun
(London).

MELVILLE, JAMES (1829): Diary 1556-
1601 (Edinburgh).

MONTGOMERIE, WILLIAM (1947): 'Tam o'
Shanter' in William Montgomerie
(ed.): Robert Burns (Glasgow), pp.
70-84.

MURE, ELIZABETH (1854): 'Remarks on
the change of manners in Scotland
during the 18th century', in Selec-
tions from the Papers of Mure of
Caldwell, 2 vols (Glasgow).

NAISMITH, JOHN (1795): Observations
on the Different Breeds of Sheep
(Edinburgh).

The New Statistical Account of
Scotland (1845): 15 vols
(Edinburgh).

Old Statistical Account (OSA) (see
Sinclair [1791-99]).

PATERSON, JAMES (1863-66): History of
the Counties of Ayr and Wigtown,
5 vols.

PENNANT, THOMAS (1771): A Tour in
Scotland: MDCCLXIX (Chester).

PICKEN, EBENEZER (1788): Poems and
Epistles (Paisley).

PORTER, ROY (2000): Quacks: Fakers
and Charlatans in English Medicine
(Stroud).

PRINGLE, JOHN (1759-60) 'Several
Accounts of the fiery meteor, which
appeared on Sunday the 15th
November, 1758', Philosophical
Transactions, 51, 218-59; and 'Some
remarks on the several accounts of
the fiery meteor', ibid., 250-74.

RAMSAY, ALLAN (1945-74): Works, 6 vols
(Edinburgh).

REID, THOMAS (1922-23): 'The Lee Penny', in *Proceedings of the Society of Antiquaries of Scotland*, 57, 112-19.

RIDDELL, MARIA (1792): *Voyages to the Madeira, and Leeward Caribbean Islands* (Edinburgh).

ROBERTSON, J. LOGIE (ed.) (1904): *Poetical Works of Robert Burns*, (Oxford).

ROBERTSON, WILLIAM (1908): *Ayrshire: its History and Historic Families*, 2 vols (Kilmarnock).

ROY, WILLIAM (1777): 'Experiments and observations ... in order to obtain a rule for measuring heights with the barometer', *Philosophical Transactions* 67, 653-78.

SCOT, REGINALD (1972): *The Discoverie of Witchcraft* (New York).

SCOTT, WALTER (1830): *Letters on Demonology and Witchcraft* (London).
_____ (1824): *Redgauntlet* (Edinburgh).

Scottish National Dictionary (see Grant and Murison).

SILLAR, DAVID (1789): *Poems* (Kilmarnock).

SINCLAIR, JOHN (ed.) (1791-99): *The Statistical Account of Scotland*, 21 vols (Edinburgh).

SMITH, GRAHAM (1989): *Robert Burns the Exciseman* (Ayr).

SMOUT, T. C. (1969): *A History of the Scottish People 1560-1830* (Glasgow).

SPROTT, GAVIN (1987): *Robert Burns, Farmer* (Edinburgh).
_____ (1996): *Robert Burns: Pride and Passion* (Edinburgh).

STEVEN, HELEN J. (1899): *Old Cumnock* (Kilmarnock).

STEVENSON, ROBERT LOUIS (1950): *Collected Poems* (London).

STEVENSON, WILLIAM (1880-81): 'Notes on the antiquities of the islands of Colonsay and Oransay', *Proceedings of the Society of Antiquaries of Scotland*, 15, 118-47.

SULLIVAN, RICHARD JOSEPH (1780): *Observations Made on a Tour Through Parts of England, Scotland and Wales* (London).

THIN, ROBERT (1938): 'Medical quacks in Edinburgh in the seventeenth and eighteenth centuries', in *Book of the Old Edinburgh Club*, 22, pp. 132-59.

THOMSON, DUNCAN (1975): *Painting in Scotland, 1570-1650* (Edinburgh).

URQUHART, H. J. (2002): 'Sawney Bean: myth or myth', *Ayrshire Notes*, no. 23, pp. 15-18.

WALKER, PATRICK (1727): *Some Remarkable Passages in the Life and Death of these Three Famous Worthies ...* (Edinburgh).

WILSON, WILLIAM (1904): *Folk Lore and Genealogies of Uppermost Nithsdale* (Dumfries).

WODROW, ROBERT (1842-43): *Analecta*, 4 vols (Edinburgh).

WOOD, JOHN MAXWELL (1911): *Witchcraft and Superstitions Record in south-west Scotland* (Dumfries).

YOUNG, ALEX F. (1998): *The Encyclopaedia of Scottish Executions* (Orpington).

Further Reading
and Exploring

Biography of Robert Burns

JAMES MACKAY (1992): *Burns: A Biography of Robert Burns.* The most scrupulous attempt to separate fact from fancy in the life of Burns.

Studies of Robert Burns's writings in the context of his life

ROBERT CRAWFORD (2009): *The Bard: Robert Burns, a Biography* (London).

DAVID DAICHES (1966): *Robert Burns: the Poet,* 2nd edition.

HANS HECHT (1936, reprinted): *Robert Burns: the Man and His Work.*

GAVIN SPROTT (1987): *Robert Burns, Farmer;* and *Robert Burns: Pride and Passion* (1996).

JOHN STRAWHORN (1959): *Ayrshire at the Time of Burns.* A collection of source material.

Additional publications

PETER BURKE (2009): *Popular Culture in Early Modern Europe,* 3rd edition. An academic classic.

The Compendium of Scottish Ethnology, 14 vols (2003-). A mass of historical background to daily life in Scotland.

EDWARD J. COWAN and LIZANNE HENDERSON (2002): 'The last of the witches? The survival of Scottish witch belief', in Julian Goodare (ed.): *The Scottish Witch-Hunt in Context;* and *Scottish Fairy Belief: a History* (2001); and 'Burns and superstition' in Kenneth Simpson (ed.) (1997): *Love and Liberty: Robert Burns, a bicentenary celebration.*

JOHN MACTAGGART (1824, reprinted 1981): *The Scottish Gallovidian Encyclopedia.*

KENNETH SIMPSON (1994): *Robert Burns;* and Gerard Carruthers (2006): *Robert Burns.* Two valuable modern short interpretations of the poems.

WALTER SCOTT (1830): *Letters on Demonology and Witchcraft.*

Standard texts

JAMES KINSLEY (ed.) (1968): *The Poems and Songs of Robert Burns,* 3 vols. A scholarly edition: the third volume consists of notes on the first two.

J. DE LANCY FERGUSON and G. ROSS ROY (eds) (1985): *The Letters of Robert Burns,* 2nd edition.

J. LOGIE ROBERTSON (ed.) (1904): *Poetical Works of Robert Burns,* (Oxford). Robertson was a competent poet in the Scots language, writing as 'Hugh Haliburton'.

Web resources

- Burns Country
  http://www.robertburns.org/
  Includes the texts of all the poems but not the songs, and a good encyclopedia.

- The National Burns Collection
  http://burnsscotland.com
  A database of 36,000 items relating to Burns – books, manuscripts, objects and art.

- Roy's map of Scotland, made in 1747-55 (original in The British Library):
  http://www.nls.uk/maps/roy/index.html
  There are other 18th-century maps of Scotland on the same website.

- SCRAN
  http://scran.ac.uk
  A resource of over 360,000 images, film and sound clips from museums, galleries and the media, with an emphasis on Scottish culture.

Places to visit

AYRSHIRE

- ALLOWAY
  The National Trust for Scotland site includes the cottage where the poet was born, the Burns Monument (1823) and gardens, Kirk Alloway (with a small number of interesting headstones), and Brig o' Doon. In addition, the Robert Burns Birthplace Museum, which will display the most important Burns collection in the world, will open in 2010. Nearby is the Rozelle House Gallery which owns a number of Alexander Goudie's splendid paintings; they are available in book form in *Alexander Goudie's Tam o' Shanter* (2008).

- AYR
  The Auld Kirk beside the River Ayr, and 200 yards downstream the massive, crooked Auld Brig.

- KILMARNOCK
  A replica of the printing press which produced the Kilmarnock edition is in the Dick Institute, and there are other items of memorabilia at Dean Castle.

- MAUCHLINE
  The Burns House Museum, beside the kirk where 'The Holy Fair' is set and the tower where Burns's friend Gavin Hamilton lived; Mossgiel is a mile away.

- RIVER AYR
  The River Ayr walk goes 'From Glenbuck down to the Ratton-Quay', as Burns puts it in 'The Brigs of Ayr.' It is a splendid journey across moorland, through deep wooded gorges, and along holms beside the river. It goes close to Mauchline and Mossgiel.

- TARBOLTON AND KIRKOSWALD

  The Batchelors' Club, Tarbolton, and Soutar Johnnie's Cottage, Kirkoswald, both in the care of the National Trust for Scotland. The latter is opposite the kirkyard which has the best selection in Ayrshire of headstones with carved symbols.

DUMFRIESSHIRE

- DUMFRIES

  The Globe Inn, the Robert Burns Centre, and Burns House, where the poet died. The last has important memorabilia; and material on Dumfries in Burns's time is to be found in Dumfries Museum.

  http://www.futuremuseum.co.uk

- ELLISLAND

  Where Burns farmed and wrote most of Tam o' Shanter.

Other related places

- WESTER KITTOCHSIDE, NEAR EAST KILBRIDE

  www.nms.ac.uk/our_museums/museum_of_rural_life.aspx

  National Museum of Rural Life (part of National Museums Scotland), where one gallery shows how farming was changing in Burns's period.

- EDINBURGH

  www.nms.ac.uk/our_museums/national_museum.aspx

  National Museum of Scotland (part of National Museums Scotland), with a gallery on life in 18th-century Scotland.

Index